# DRAFTING A CONSTITUTION FOR A NATION OR REPUBLIC EMERGING INTO FREEDOM

## BERNARD H. SIEGAN

SECOND EDITION

**George Mason University Press**
Fairfax, Virginia

Copyright © 1994 by
**George Mason University Press**
4400 University Drive
Fairfax, VA 22030

All rights reserved
Printed in the United States of America
British Cataloging in Publication Information Available

Distributed by arrangement with
University Publishings Associates,$^{SM}$ Inc.

4720 Boston Way
Lanham, Maryland 20706

3 Henrietta Street
London WC2E 8LU England

**Library of Congress Cataloging-in-Publication Data**

Siegan, Bernard H.
Drafting a constitution for a nation or republic emerging into freedom
/ Bernard H. Siegan.
p.   cm.
Includes bibliographical references and indexes.
1. Constitutional law.   2. Separation of powers.   3. Civil rights.
I. Title.
K3165.S545   1994   342'.02—dc20 [342.22]   94-2283   CIP

ISBN 0-913969-70-2 (cloth : acid-free paper)

Second Edition

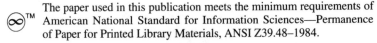

# Contents

# Introduction

The people who inhabited the thirteen American colonies in the late eighteenth century differ greatly in history, origin, and culture from those people who today occupy the vast expanses of Eastern and Central Europe and adjoining Asian areas. The differences between the two groups appear enormous except, of course, in one respect: biology. The human species has wants, desires and needs common to it wherever it exists.

Accordingly, is there enough similarity between the inhabitants of the Western world of the late Eighteenth Century and those of the nations and republics emerging from communism so that the American constitutional experience can serve as a model for these lands? The people who ratified the United States Constitution were then the beneficiaries of centuries of common law experience. Limitations on government powers and protection of liberties were part of their tradition and influenced their culture. But the human need for freedom was obviously not unique to them. The rejection of communism in major portions of the world constitutes a strong message that the Hobbesian concept of the all-powerful state is not consistent with the human condition. After long experiencing it, millions of people have found communism incapable of satisfying their aspirations.[1]

Moreover, while we cannot be certain about their political preferences, recent elections in the former communist nations disclose the people's desire to limit substantially the power of government. In this respect, they are no different than the Americans of a much earlier time. In both situations, the people insisted on retaining a large measure of autonomy over their lives—an essential foundation for a constitutional system dedicated to the rule of law.

When in August, 1990, I first suggested to Andrei Lukanov, then prime minister of Bulgaria, that the United States Constitution should be the major source for the new Bulgarian Constitution, his reply was largely negative. He stated that people in his part of the world wanted a parliamentary system where the legislative body is supreme. The separation of powers would inhibit the people's control over their own destiny. As the discussion turned to foreign investment which he agreed would be difficult to obtain if the parliament had power to confiscate it, he began to reconsider his views. The idea of a separate constitutional court with the power to protect the right of private ownership and other liberties became more acceptable.[2]

I encountered almost the same experience in discussions I held in the summer and fall of 1990 with more than two dozen Bulgarian officials, judges, and lawyers. In time, most of them agreed as to the desirability of the separation of powers. The constitution recently adopted by the Bulgarian parliament provides for the separation of powers, a constitutional court, and numerous protections for private rights.[3]

Only the passage of time will reveal whether the Bulgarians succeed in their present political objectives. Benjamin Franklin's observation at the conclusion of the American Constitutional Convention of 1787 is worth noting. When asked, "What have we got a republic or a monarchy?" He answered, "A republic, if you can keep it."[4]

During my discussions I learned that Bulgarians are not as respectful of judges as we are in this country. Many consider judges to be almost on the order of government clerks and some were appalled at the thought that judges could nullify laws passed by the National Assembly, the representative of all the people. The idea of a specially selected group of lawyers that would constitute a constitutional court—confined to interpreting the constitution—overcame much of this concern.

The new Bulgarian constitution creates such a court. It also separates the powers of the President and the Assembly but not in the manner of the United States Constitution. While the Bulgarian President is separately elected, has many executive powers, and can require the assembly to reconsider bills it passes, the parliament selects the prime minister and other ministers of government. Thus, while the division of powers and checks and balances exist under their document, they are far less pronounced than under the United States Constitution.

The success of constitutional government depends on the willingness of people to accept and be bound by legitimate governmental decisions that they greatly fear or intensely dislike. Except for the Civil War period, the people of the United States generally have honored the exercise of power by the three major branches of government. Indeed, the Supreme Court has ruled in the most controversial areas in favor of relatively small minorities and against the great majority. Nonetheless, this nation has never had to impose force to implement the court's will. Counting the ten amendments of the Bill of Rights as one, the Constitution has been amended only seventeen times in over 200 years. By tradition and culture, Americans are prepared for the assertion of legitimate government power to support highly disfavored groups and ideas.

The emerging nations and republics are largely devoid of this experience. It is uncertain how the rule of law will fare in their midst. However, these countries have little choice in the matter. Having committed to economies based on private market forces, they must now legally secure these systems; otherwise they jeopardize their economic viability without which freedom cannot exist.

Contemporary experience is persuasive that the emerging nations will benefit from a market economy. This is the record of nations throughout the world, many of whom have minimum background in free enterprise. These nations vary in history and culture and include: Taiwan, South Korea, Thailand, Iceland, Malaysia, Indonesia, Mauritius and Botswana. In recent years, the South and Central American countries of Chile, Argentina, Bolovia, Paraguay, Ecuador, Mexico and El Salvador have begun to pursue free economic policies by removing economic regulations, privatizing businesses and reducing trade barriers, with considerable success as of this writing.

Culture may be a factor in a nation's economy but far less so than economic incentive. The existence of market incentives accounts for the prosperity of Taiwan, West Germany and South Korea. The lack of such incentives explains the economic failures of China, East Germany and North Korea. Changing to a market system can make an enormous difference. Initiated in 1978, the progressive decollectivization of Chinese agricultural land "prompted a dramatic surge in productivity . . . China was transformed from a net importer of food to an actual exporter." This agricultural rebirth "stimulated growth in the output of Chinese rural industry, which increased by a staggering 400% between 1981 and 1986 and which grew by a further 36 percent in 1987 alone."[5]

As the foremost legal document, the Constitutions of the emerging states must reflect and advance their existing commitment to a free society. In the following pages, I shall set forth terms and provisions that I believe a constitution dedicated to the maintenance of a free society should contain, together with the rationale and philosophy behind them. A suggested model constitution follows (Appendix I) together with a copy of the Constitution of the United States (Appendix II).

# 1

# United States Constitutional Experience

## I Authority versus Liberty

A major concern of constitution framers is to determine how much power government should possess. For the communist leaders, the answer was simple. Government should have absolute power. The answer of the framers of the United States Constitution was quite different. The state exists for the benefit of the people; the human being does not exist for the benefit of the state. Government should have only as much power as necessary to secure the people's liberty and property. Believing they had achieved this goal, the framers did not include a bill of rights in the original constitution ratified in 1788. Thus, in the ratification period, Alexander Hamilton (a framer and major political leader) argued against adding a bill of rights because he thought it superfluous. The government was of such modest character, he wrote, that it posed no threat to individual liberties.[6]

The U.S. Constitution was written at a time when the ideas of natural rights and limited government prevailed in intellectual circles. The writings of the English philosopher John Locke (1632–1704) and legal commentators Edward Coke (1552–1634) and William Blackstone (1723–1780) were highly influential. According to Locke, organized society is based on a social compact defining the powers accorded government and limiting its sovereignty over the individual. The legislature may not deprive the individual of fundamental rights—first, because the social compact does not provide a government with this power, and second, because government's purpose is to play a fiduciary role in safeguarding and enhancing those rights. Limitations on governmental powers are central to Locke's theory.

It cannot be supposed that [individuals] should intend, had they a power so to do, to give to any one, or more, an absolute arbitrary power over their persons and estates, and put a force into the magistrate's hand to execute his unlimited will arbitrarily upon them. This were to put themselves into a worse condition than the state of nature, wherein they had a liberty to defend their right against the injuries of others, and were upon equal terms of force to maintain it, whether invaded by a single man or many in combination.[7]

The [government] cannot take from any man any part of his property without his own consent. For the preservation of property being the end of government, and that for which men enter into society, it necessarily supposes and requires that the people should have property, without which they must be supposed to lose that by entering into society, which was the end for which they entered into it, too gross an absurdity for any man to own.[8]

Coke believed that positive laws are subject to the higher laws of "common right and reason" and should provide a foundation for the creation of limited government under which the courts, through judicial review, would be able to preserve the social compact's essential character.

Blackstone wrote about the laws of England and viewed them as securing individual autonomy. He identified as absolute the rights of life, liberty and property. Blackstone believed that the principal end of society is to protect the enjoyment of these absolute rights, which were subject only to "[r]estraints in themselves so gentle and moderate, as will appear upon further inquiry, that no man of sense or probity would wish to seek them slackened." To vindicate these rights when violated, the people were entitled, first, to seek judicial relief; second, to petition the king and parliament; and lastly, to use armed force.[9]

When the United States Constitution was framed in 1787, the American people thought about government much in the way the people of Eastern Europe do at present. They had experienced tyranny and sought a political system that maximized liberty. The United States Constitution reflects this perspective. For the framers of the Constitution, the separation and enumeration of powers, checks and balances between government branches, and judicial review to secure liberties were political and economic ideas that would safeguard the individual in his personal, business, or professional life from government oppression. Society would benefit because liberty was regarded as providing the greatest encouragement to human progress. The same reasoning remains applicable today. The people of the United States rely on freedom to advance understanding and culture as well as to supply food, clothing and shelter. No better means has yet been devised to serve these needs.

The essence of American constitutional thinking is that the forces of production, conservation and creativity rest principally in the intellectual and commercial marketplaces and not in government. Thus, it may be true that intellectuals and entrepreneurs act largely in their own self interest, but probably no more so than government officials, and their endeavors are much more oriented to furthering the general public good.[10]

## II  Separation of Powers

The form and character of government is an important consideration in the framing of a constitution. Libertarian societies differ in the structures of their governments. Some have selected the parliamentary system and others the separation of powers system. Probably most contemporary constitutions combine elements of both. The United States is the nation that first created the separation system in 1787 and still maintains it over 200 years later. Under it, the people of the United States are supreme in their sovereignty except that they must always defer to persons exercising their fundamental rights.

The adoption of a constitution is a most important political event in the history of a country. In this process, the people relinquish their rights to a body that will thereafter be able to exercise control over them. People should be most concerned about this grant of power for several reasons: (1) liberty is a normal condition for humans without which the value of life is reduced, (2) individuals freely exercising their creativity, ingenuity and productivity have accounted for society's greatest advances, and (3) the government may use its power unwisely or tyrannically. Nonetheless, few disagree that government is required to protect the people from their own excesses and from the violence of domestic and foreign interests.

Two-hundred years ago, Americans faced with this dilemma of liberty and authority sought an obvious solution: to create a government that would be powerful enough to protect them but not powerful enough to oppress them. James Madison, the most influential framer of the United States Constitution, described the problem in this manner: "In framing a government which is to be administered by men over men, the great difficulty lies in this: You must first enable the government to control the governed; and in the next place, oblige it to control itself."[11]

The people of early America rejected the parliamentary system since it vested almost all governmental powers in one body. They believed that when unlimited power is lodged either in a king or a parliament regardless how well-intentioned either may be, there is considerable risk that it will be exercised tyrannically.

Instead, the framers of the United States Constitution chose a system that fractionalized government power into legislative, executive and judicial branches. If governmental power is divided so that a particular policy can be implemented only by a combination of *legislative* enactment, *executive* implementation, and *judicial* interpretation, no group of persons will be able to impose its unchecked will.[12]

As Madison explained,

> The accumulation of all powers, legislative, executive, and judiciary, in the same hands, whether of one, a few, or many, and whether hereditary, self-appointed, or elective, may justly be pronounced the very definition of tyranny.[13]

In addition to functioning separately, each of the branches of the United States government has certain powers to restrain the others. The purpose is to create substantial checks and balances on the exercise of governmental authority. Thus, the Senate must consent by majority vote to major appointments (including Supreme Court and other federal judges) made by the President, and must by two-thirds vote agree to treaties negotiated by the President. Congress establishes courts of lesser authority than the Supreme Court and has power to control the judicial appeals process. The President has the power of veto over Congressional legislation which can only be overridden by a two-thirds vote of Congress. The President appoints Supreme Court and all federal judges, but again only with the consent of the Senate. Congress has the power to declare war and fund it, but the President is Commander-in-Chief. In short, the Constitutional objective is to diffuse and disperse authority to make it very difficult for any group to obtain substantial power over the American government.

In a 1983 decision strongly supportive of the separation system, Chief Justice Burger asserted that its requirements are a small price to pay for the benefits of freedom:

> The choices we discern as having been made in the Constitutional Convention impose burdens on governmental processes that often seem clumsy, inefficient, even unworkable, but those hard choices were consciously made by men who had lived under a form of government that permitted arbitrary governmental acts to go unchecked. . . . With all the obvious flaws of delay, untidiness, and potential for abuse, we have not yet found a better way to preserve freedom than by making the exercise of power subject to the carefully crafted restraints spelled out in the Constitution.[14]

As Burger suggests, a unitary or parliamentary government may come to decisions more quickly but at times with great cost to individual dignity and autonomy. Moreover, recent world history confirms that insofar as the advancement of society is concerned, freedom towers over authority.[15] The "delay, untidiness and potential for abuse" Burger mentions, is more than overcome by the material and intellectual rewards of freedom.

Clearly, the passage of legislation is difficult under the separation system that exists in the United States, as recent history discloses. President George Bush vetoed over two dozen measures passed by the Congress, which failed in every instance except one to override him. This result could not occur under a system in which the parliament is the supreme and absolute governmental authority in the nation. Throughout American history legislation has often failed because of a presidential veto or a Supreme Court decision striking it down.

Nevertheless, there has been little criticism of the separation system in the United States. Americans may criticize individual presidential or judicial actions but rarely the division of authority. The fifty states of the union also utilize the separation system. The people generally agree that the President's right to veto legislation leads to better, sounder and more democratically based laws, as was expressed at this nation's founding by Alexander Hamilton:

> The oftener the measure is brought under examination, the greater the diversity in the situations of those who are to examine it, the less must be the danger of those errors which flow from want of due deliberation, or of those missteps which proceed from the contagion of some common passion or interest. It is far less probable that culpable views of any kind should infect all the parts of the government at the same moment and in relation to the same object than that they should by turns govern and mislead every one of them.[16]

Oppressive measures may still pass the executive and legislative branches but, Hamilton asserted, are less likely to succeed at the judicial branch:

> The complete independence of the courts of justice is peculiarly essential in a limited Constitution. By a limited Constitution, I understand one which contains certain specified exceptions to the legislative authority; . . . Limitations of this kind can be preserved in practice no other way than through the medium of courts of justice, whose duty it must be to declare all acts contrary to the manifest tenor of the Constitution void. Without this, all the reservations of particular rights or privileges would amount to nothing.[17]

# 2
# Powers of and Restraints on the Legislature and President

## I  Confining the Legislature

In a system where the powers are separate, the lawmaking body must share power with the executive and judiciary. While originally the primary purpose of constitutional government in Western societies was to restrain the monarch, the primary modern purpose seems to be to restrain the legislature. When the United States Constitution was framed a commonly held belief was that the greatest peril to liberty comes from expanding powers of legislative bodies:

> [T]here was more concern as to the restrictions under which governments should operate than as to the functions to be performed. Governments were to be prohibited from interfering with freedom of person, security of property, freedom of speech and of religion. The guaranty of liberty was, therefore, to give the rulers as little power as possible and then to surround them with numerous restrictions—to balance power against power.[18]

James Madison and most other framers of the Constitution believed the legislatures harbored serious threats to freedom. Consider, for example, his observations in *Federalist No. 48:* "The legislative department is everywhere extending the sphere of its activity, and drawing all power into its impetuous vortex.. . . ." "[I]t is against the enterprising ambition of this department that the people ought to indulge all their jealousy and exhaust all their precautions."[19]

Other leading Framers were no less apprehensive about lawmakers. Hamilton condemned the state legislatures for failing to safeguard commercial rights.[20] Gouverneur Morris found in every state legislative department "excesses [against] personal liberty private property [and] personal safety,"[21] and Edmund Randolph presented the Virginia Plan to the Convention to overcome the "turbulence and follies of democracy."[22]

These sentiments are obviously not unique to the American experience. Accordingly, lawmakers should be fairly selected, should observe fair and appropriate process in their deliberations, and should not have authority to oppress the people or control matters in which they have no competence.

Across the world, legislatures are elected under either a majority or party proportional vote or both. Once they are in office lawmakers should be obligated to follow adequate process to assure that the laws they pass implement their intention. Before they vote on bills, committees must study and pass on them and lawmakers must always be aware of their status on the legislative calendar. To avoid deals or compromises between different interests, a bill must not embrace more than one subject which should be expressed in its title. Otherwise, arrangements can be made between supporters of different positions to achieve a majority which would not be possible for either position. Likewise, appropriations bills should concern only spending of monies and should not mandate any other action or conduct.

Legislatures should be restricted in their power over legitimate private activity and conduct. The United States Constitution prohibits legislatures from passing laws that inflict punishment on named individuals or easily ascertainable members of a group.[23] Government should not deny or deprive persons of their rights unless it has strong justification for doing so. In the absence of such reason, government has no basis for reducing individual initiative and opportunity upon which society is dependent for advancement and achievement.

Legislatures are not competent to control most matters in the private sector. In a society seeking to maximize individual opportunity, government should not own or operate property except when necessary to provide essential services and facilities that would not otherwise be obtainable. The province of government, centrally or through its various branches, is to govern, and this does not include as a general matter ownership or operation of property or investment. (See Chapter 6.)

The legislature should not be authorized to pass retroactive laws; all laws should be made to commence in *futuro*.[24] The justification for this rule is both moral and pragmatic. It is generally immoral for government to penalize a person who has acted in reliance on existing law either by subsequently making the action illegal or subsequently depriving the person of rights acquired by the action. Predictability of law protects the individual from arbitrary government rules and rulers. In the criminal area, retroactive laws are universally condemned as *ex post facto* laws. (An *ex post facto* law is one that renders an act punishable in a manner in which it was not punishable when it was committed.) Retroactive civil laws are not more acceptable inasmuch as the same principles are involved. Consider Chancellor James Kent's observations in this regard:

> [T]here is no distinction in principle, nor any recognized in practice, between a law punishing a person criminally, for a past innocent act, or punishing him civilly by divesting him of a lawfully acquired right. The distinction consists only in the degree of the oppression, and history teaches us that the government which can deliberately violate the one right, soon ceases to regard the other.[25]

Retroactive civil laws are pragmatically unwise as well. By imposing new restraints, they raise the risk of economic failure and thereby discourage ownership and investment. There are times when the security of the state and its people require passage of retroactive laws. These exceptions would include laws or regulations enacted in conditions of emergency for the purpose of preserving law and order; laws or regulations prohibiting, regulating or abating actions or uses damaging public health and safety; and laws or regulations causing the value of property or a commercial venture to be reduced a relatively small percent of its market value.[26]

Legislators are continually lobbied by private groups seeking laws in their own interest. However, government should not have the power to favor particular persons or groups. The legislature should be barred from granting any private individual or group of individuals any special or exclusive right, privilege, immunity, or preference. In the United States, many private groups seek legislation in their own favor and quite often succeed in these efforts. Congress and state legislatures disguise such maneuvers by claiming the law was adopted to serve solely specified public benefits. However, if its purpose was to serve the special interests of certain persons to the detriment of others, it should not be considered as valid. This problem is a major one for representative government and will be discussed in greater detail subsequently in relation to regulatory legislation (chapters 5 and 6).

Under the suggested model constitution set forth in Appendix I, the powers of the legislature are considerably limited. These limitations on government authority should not be a cause for concern—particularly in the emerging states. Communist leaders passed or imposed countless laws to better the life of their constituents and were ever ready to adopt more "in the public interest." As a result, the communist nations had an abundance of laws, but, as it turned out, never of food, clothing and shelter. The problem was that communism identified the public good with ever greater government authority.

By contrast, the market oriented countries have achieved much more benefits for the people by following an opposite principle, equating the public interest with individual freedom. Capitalist countries such as the United States rely on individual ingenuity, creativity and productivity to improve and advance society. History confirms that free minds, hearts, and bodies account for the greatest societal achievements.

## II  Powers of the President

In a government based on separation of powers, the President is the chief executive officer of the nation, charged with implementing the nation's laws. In the United States, the office also includes substantial legislative authority such as the power of the veto and the formulation and conduct of foreign policy. (To be binding, treaties negotiated by the President must be confirmed by two-thirds vote of the Senate.)

### A.  The President's Power of Veto

The desirability of a veto power similar to the one given the American President is a quite controversial issue in the emerging states. Under the United States Constitution, the President may veto a measure passed by the Congress, and this veto can only be overridden by a two-thirds vote of that body. Critics contend this veto gives monarchial or dictatorial power to the President, while supporters reply that it is a reasonable and desirable part of the legislative process. The executive veto is an accepted institution in the United States, and while its particular application may raise considerable protest, the principle generally does not. Every state in the nation provides for a similar power or the more specific line item veto (explained in Chapter 6 under III "Provisions on Taxing and Spending"). This record of success warrants serious consideration of the executive veto by contemporary constitution draftsmen.

As a limitation on the legislature, the president's veto is an essential element of the separation system. Europeans, however, currently are more favorably disposed toward the parliamentary system on the theory that it is the most democratic form of government. Nevertheless, they are willing to depart from it in two respects: judicial review, and some forms of discretionary executive power, such as a very limited veto and the power to grant pardons. As to selecting members of the legislature, contemporary European political leaders accept majority or proportional voting or a combination of both. The objective is to make certain that the legislature is truly representative of the people.

"Every person's vote should be worth the same" is a universally accepted idea in democratic societies but one very difficult to achieve (see chapter 6). Obviously, voting districts should be equal in population, yet this result does not ensure that the boundary lines have not created minorities in the districts by dividing up large voting blocs. Thus American civil rights litigation has shown that the drawing of the boundary lines between districts may make several smaller blocs out of one racial or ethnic bloc. For example, to augment the voting strength of black voters, a New York redistricting plan divided an Hasidic Jewish neighborhood that had formerly been included in a single election district. When this action was challenged, the United States Supreme Court upheld it as complying with the Voting Rights Act of 1965, which was intended to prevent redistricting that disadvantaged black voters.[27] Passage of the act itself acknowledges the difficulties inherent in securing equal participation in the electoral process.

Proportionalists insist that no matter how equal the districts are in population, minorities will be submerged in many districts and as a result will be unable to obtain fair representation. Only by giving minority interests proportional representation can the legislature be truly representative.

Majoritarians reply that proportional representation gives minorities excessive power in a legislature where no party has a majority and needs the minorities' vote to obtain it. Indeed, there is little universality on what constitutes a truly representative legislature. The two-thirds vote required by the President's veto under the United States Constitution seeks to make certain that the Congress' vote on a particular measure truly represents the people's will.

A president in a separated government is neither dictator nor monarch; he or she represents and is always accountable to the people. A president is not likely to exercise the veto unless the matter is of major importance. Nor is he or she likely to incur the legislature's displeasure by vetoing a measure unless the issue warrants it. Thus, essentially the executive veto is consistent with the highest aspirations of democratic decision making, requiring that in major matters a clear majority of the people's representatives determine the nation's destiny.

## B. Power of appointment

Under the United States separation system of government, the major holders of executive power are appointed by the President, and they together with the President constitute the cabinet. The President shares the appointment power with Congress to the extent that the latter must confirm major individual appointments. Congress writes the rules by which cabinet departments must operate and provides their funds, but cabinet members and their departments will largely reflect the political and philosophical views of the President.

The cabinet has a different basis in a parliamentary system. Since there is no separate executive branch under it, the nation's highest executive officials are appointed and largely controlled by the legislature. The problem with this form of governing relates to the monopoly of power. Government officials are less likely to be arbitrary in the exercise of power if they are beholden to two separate branches of government, rather than to one.

## C.  Power to pardon wrongdoers

The United States Constitution invests the President with the power to pardon those convicted of crimes against the federal government. This power has been interpreted to include the commutation of punishment, granting of amnesty to specified classes or groups, and placing conditions on the pardon. This power operates as another restraint on governmental authority over people.

## D.  The Role of a President Under a Parliamentary System

To be sure, a nation need not follow the American separation of powers concept to grant a separately elected president substantial powers. For a nation utilizing the parliamentary system, providing the president with such authority would still obtain many benefits of divided government. Consideration should be given to empowering the president to engage in critical governmental decisions that are not ordinarily considered appropriate for this office under a parliamentary system. The French constitution, which provides for direct election of the president, with a seven-year term for this office, offers guidance in this respect.[28] Under it, the French President has the following powers:

1. He appoints the premier, and other members of the government upon recommendation of the premier (art. 8).

2. He can require the parliament to reconsider a law it has passed, or certain parts of it (art. 10).

3. He can dissolve once a year the national assembly, requiring new elections to be held for it (art. 2). This is the branch of parliament elected by direct suffrage. The President and cabinet are not affected by this provision enabling them to govern without any restraints imposed by the said legislative body.

4. He is commander of the armed forces (art. 15).

5. He may exercise by decree emergency powers that limit constitutional powers (art. 16).

6.   He possesses the power of pardon (art. 17).

7.   On the recommendation of the government or the Parliament, he may call a referendum dealing with the organization of the government and several other important national matters (art. 11).

By themselves, these are extensive powers. However, they should be considered as one part of the package of government, which also includes legislative and judicial bodies that also have substantial powers. To prevent the president's abuse of these powers, a constitution should accord checks and balances to the other branches, such as the legislative power of impeachment, required legislative consent for the exercise of certain powers, and judicial review.

# 3
# Administrative Agencies

In the modern world, a fourth branch of government has arisen that for a great many people is as powerful as any of the other three. This branch consists of the agencies and commissions created by the legislature to administer regulatory legislation. Businesses and ordinary people consult and confront these governmental bodies continually in matters of manufacturing, commerce, agriculture, zoning, building, housing, licenses, police, social security, welfare, environment, health, etc. These agencies and commissions are always subject to the constitutional standards protecting the people, and although not elected should be subject as much as possible to democratic control.

A constitutional court should have jurisdiction to consider complaints that the administrative bodies have violated constitutional terms, either procedurally or substantively. Administrative bodies are creatures of the legislature and have no more power than the legislature that created them. Nor should they have legislative powers. Under the American system, a legislature cannot delegate its legislative powers to any other group. The theory behind this rule is that in selecting candidates for office, the voters chose specific individuals to make political decisions. They did not grant this power to the unidentified persons who compose the agencies and commissions. It is basic that the laws be made by the persons elected for that purpose and not by appointees who have no responsibility to the voters. As John Locke stated almost three centuries ago:

> The power of the *Legislative* being derived from the people by a positive voluntary Grant and Institution, can be no other, than what the positive Grant conveyed, which being only to make *Laws,* and not to make *Legisla-*

*tors,* the *Legislative* can have no power to transfer their authority of making Laws, and place it in other hands.[29]

A major problem of administrative law is that regulatory legislation establishing administrative bodies often is not precise as to the power of the body, and may be sufficiently ambiguous to enable it to exercise legislative powers. As U.S. Supreme Court Justice Brennan has explained,

> [F]ormulation of policy is a legislature's primary responsibility, entrusted to it by the electorate, and to the extent Congress delegates authority under indefinite standards, this policy-making function is passed on to other agencies, often not answerable or responsive in the same degree to the people.[30]

The problem is worthy of constitutional concern. The legislature may not delegate its legislative powers to a commission but should set forth the general rules under which the commission should proceed, with a view to making orders in particular situations. The role of the administrative body is to adapt legislation to contemporary conditions involving details with which the legislature cannot deal directly.[31]

> "The true distinction . . . is between the delegation of power to make the law, which necessarily involves a discretion as to what it shall be, and conferring authority or discretion *as to its execution,* to be exercised under and in pursuance of the law. The first cannot be done; to the latter no valid objection can be made."[32]

Obviously, the more power exercised by the legislature, the more inescapable is the problem of administrative authority. An important consideration for the legislature when it contemplates regulation is that as a result of it, many important decisions will be made affecting life, liberty and property by politically appointed administrators who are not subject to voter approval.

# 4
# The Judiciary

## I    The Judicial Function

The protection of both liberty and authority requires an independent judiciary powerful enough to monitor the legislature and executive to assure compliance with the constitution. The judiciary in the United States has the power to annul legislation that is unconstitutional and at times to require compensation for unconstitutional actions. Aggrieved parties must have reasonable access to the courts to protect their rights. When interpreting the Constitution, the judiciary has only the power to negate laws, not the power to impose them.

This power of final judicial review may be lodged in a supreme court of general jurisdiction (such as the United States Supreme Court) or in a constitutional court limited in jurisdiction solely to constitutional issues (such as the German Constitutional Court). Because of its great powers, members of such courts should be most carefully selected. In the United States, members of the nine-person Supreme Court are appointed for life by the President with the concurrence of the Senate. By contrast, the French Constitutional Council also consists of nine members but they are limited to nine-year terms of office. One-third of the membership is renewed every three years. The President of the Republic, President of the National Assembly and President of the Senate each appoint three members.[33]

While likely to adopt it, Eastern Europeans are reported to be apprehensive about judicial review of constitutional disputes. They seem to be more comfortable relying on the legislature rather than the judiciary to protect their rights.[34] The problem with such thinking is that individual rights are immunities from the legislative power. Presumably the legislature has already exercised the protective function—that is, securing liberty—in passing legislation and there is nothing more for it to do in this regard. In considering challenges to the legislation it has passed, the lawmakers would be acting in their own behalf. Authors of even the most restrictive laws are not likely to believe that the laws are unreasonable.

The responsibility for protecting rights belongs to a separate branch of government, the judiciary. Among other things, owners and investors should be confident that the legislature will not be permitted to confiscate their assets. When one group wants to acquire the property or property rights of another, the legislature should not be able to aid them in making the acquisition.[35] People should understand that in exercising their rights, they are not at the mercy of the politicians. The legislature cannot provide this assurance against itself.

The underlying assumption of many who condemn judicial review as undemocratic is that the legislature's actions tend to represent the majority's wishes. These people assume that laws brought before the courts are the results of democratically controlled processes. Experience in the United States has shown that such assumptions are highly questionable. Many measures adopted by legislatures are less representative of the people's will than are the judicial decisions striking them down. The actual operation of the election system and the legislative process makes effectuating the popular will difficult. The legislative process is seriously flawed in important respects.

First, the relationship between the will of the majority and the passage of laws is often highly tenuous. Second, many laws that are adopted are not very efficient or effective, therefore needlessly depriving some people of their liberties. Third, small special interest groups continually succeed in obtaining the passage of laws beneficial to them and harmful to much larger numbers. Fourth, even in the absence of these infirmities, legislatures still pass laws that are oppressive to some. Fifth, administrative agencies exercise much rule making authority in society, and their relationship to the popular will is remote.

The conclusion is well warranted that because of its limitations and infirmities, the legislature should not be the final legal authority in society. A strong case can be made that on many issues legislatures do not reflect the views of their constituents. The evidence is similarly persuasive that numerous critical provisions of statutes do not represent or are contrary to majoritarian will. These problems of legitimacy are compounded by problems of competency. Many legislators do not have the knowledge, understanding, incentive, or time to create efficient and effective statutes that will not unnecessarily deprive people of their liberties. Even when legislators do have the requisite qualifications, their effectiveness is limited by need for compromise and placating politically important constituents.

Of particular concern is the influence that special interest groups have on the legislative process. Small groups seeking material or ideological favors have proved to be extremely convincing in the legislative councils. Although large numbers of citizens may oppose such legislation, individually they lack the incentive and dedication to organize and lobby. This political imbalance results in the passage of laws that are disadvantageous to the general public and that may be particularly harmful to some individuals (see chapter 6).

Moreover, constituents may have several views, none of which attracts a majority. Such situations raise the well-discussed paradox of voting: a majority position results from a chance combination of first, second, and even third choices.[36]

A major premise of judicial review is that when majoritarianism – even at its theoretical best, that is rule by 50% plus one—is directly responsible for the enactment of laws, it should not be the final arbiter of all human affairs. Unless they are restrained, majorities have the power to terminate life and liberty and confiscate property. They also have the power to create dictatorships and despotic rules and processes. Alexis de Tocqueville, the famous French commentator, understood the problem quite well. He saw majoritarianism as a threat to a democratic society:

> A majority taken collectively may be regarded as a being whose opinions, and most frequently whose interests, are opposed to those of another being, which is styled a minority. If it be admitted that a man, possessing absolute power, may misuse that power by wronging his adversaries, why should a majority not be liable to the same reproach? Men are not apt to change their characters by agglomeration; nor does their patience in the presence of obstacles increase with the consciousness of their strength. And for these reasons I can never willingly invest any number of my fellow creatures with that unlimited authority which I should refuse to any of them.[37]

Alexander Hamilton said that one objective of government was to protect the weak as well as the strong. "In a society under the form of which the stronger faction can readily unite and oppress the weaker, anarchy may as truly be said to reign as in a state of nature, where the weaker individual is not secured against the violence of the stronger.[38]

Milton Friedman views majoritarianism as a threat to personal equality:

> If an elite did not have the right to impose its will on others, neither did any other group, even a majority. Every person was to be his own ruler—provided that he did not interfere with the similar right of others. Government was established to protect that right—from fellow citizens and from external threat—not to give a majority unbridled rule.[39]

The conclusion that representative government generally represents the will of a numerical majority of the population is not accurate. Large numbers of people do not and are not required, to vote. Many frequently are forbidden to do so: Persons under 18, aliens, people with criminal records, illiterates, individuals who do not register to vote and recently arrived residents. Majorities in a district are determined by the apportionment process, which determines the boundaries of an electoral area. Apportionment may divide up blocs of like-minded voters who thereafter constitute powerless minorities in various districts. These limitations in determining majorities transform true numerical majorities to something often considerably less, and seem no more onerous or unjust than those imposed by the judiciary that restrain the powers of the alleged majorities.[40] (See discussion of the President's Power of Veto in chapter 2.)

These limitations and infirmities compromise the credibility of the legislature as the representative of the political majority and therefore its entitlement to final authority over legislation. The legitimacy of imposing restraints on the public diminishes as the legislative role and purpose become less credible. Therefore, the need for the judiciary to safeguard liberties of those affected by legislation increases.

## II  Protection of Both Enumerated and Unenumerated Rights

The Constitution should protect the liberties of the people, whether or not enumerated in the Constitution, from oppressive, arbitrary, confiscatory and capricious laws and regulations.

Most important, people accused of crime should have every reasonable opportunity to prove their innocence. As a procedural matter, the burden should be on the government to prove an accused's guilt beyond a reasonable doubt. A criminal code must never be applied for political and economic purposes, nor otherwise used to punish persons innocent of wrongdoing. It must also never shield from punishment the perpetrators of crime. The imposition of penalties and punishment is solely the responsibility of the judiciary, and the legislature should have no authority in this regard except to enumerate crimes and proscribe sentences for violations of the law.

For a criminal justice system to be considered creditable and just, it must not in interpreting the laws tilt toward either the government or the alleged wrongdoer and must not impose technical barriers preventing the determination of truth. Thus, legal errors committed by the police or the prosecutors in the enforcement of the criminal code should not preclude a judge or other trier of fact from determining guilt of an accused person.

A legal code should not impose penalties on persons who abide by the law. Individuals or corporations causing injury to persons or property should be immune from criminal or tort liability for that injury if on the occasion in question they fully obeyed the relevant law. The government must not restrict the liberty of an accused person more than necessary, considering both the interests of public security and individual freedom.

The United States Constitution requires that no person accused of wrongdoing be deprived of life, liberty, or property without being afforded maximum opportunity for asserting a legal defense. The nation's law is predicated on the idea that at times freedom for the guilty is preferable to punishment for the innocent. Given this objective, both accused and convicted persons are extended a wide variety of procedural protections as set forth in the United States Constitution and judicial interpretations thereof.

A constitution should enumerate both procedural and substantive freedoms thought especially worthy of protection. Because a constitution is the result of a political process and usually remains in force for long periods of time, it is almost inevitable that not all liberties will be listed. The United States Constitution provides for this contingency in its due process clauses, which state that no person shall be deprived of life, liberty, or property without due process of law and in the ninth amendment, which states that the enumeration of certain rights shall not be construed to deny or disparage others retained by the people.

There has been considerable controversy as to the powers of the Supreme Court under the foregoing provisions. Although authored long in the past, both provisions have been interpreted to include contemporary concerns about freedom. To avoid such interpretive problems, the judiciary should be given the power to protect unenumerated as well as enumerated rights.

Moreover, as a practical matter, it is difficult to confine a court charged with enforcing liberties to the strict letter of the text. Courts in the United States (and probably elsewhere) tend to stretch the meaning of specified liberties so that they are effectively enforcing unstated protections.

The Supreme Court's experience shows that confining its authority solely to interpreting specified rights is not much of a restraint. To be sure, the designation of a right offers some protection whereas its absence provides none. However, over the years, the Justices have exercised considerable creativity in defining specified rights. For example, in 1989 the Court held that freedom of speech protects the malicious burning of the American flag.[41] The Justice who authored the famous *Griswold* opinion found that the right of privacy, which nowhere appears in the text, was established and secured by the combined meaning of the first, third, fourth and fifth amendments to the Constitution.[42]

The constitutional concern should always be about freedom in the negative sense of protecting the individual from the might of government. However, government should have no constitutional obligation to support, advance, or otherwise subsidize any private activities, even though the absence of funds may limit the enjoyment of protected rights. As Chief Justice Rehnquist has explained,

> Our cases have recognized that the Due Process Clauses generally confer no affirmative right to governmental aid, even where such aid may be necessary to secure life, liberty, or property interests of which government may not deprive the individual.[43]

The Chief Justice is correct as a matter of constitutional meaning; however, the Court has not always followed this position. In *Shapiro v. Thompson* (1969),[44] a case involving the right of travel, the Court struck down welfare statutes in the states and the District of Columbia that denied assistance to those residing there for less than one year. These jurisdictions were, as a result, required to fund a considerable number of indigents from monies that had to be obtained either from other programs or new taxes, thereby invading the spending and taxing prerogatives of legislatures.

The Court subsequently recognized the problem. In *San Antonio Independent School District v. Rodriguez* (1973)[45] the Court refused to require increased funding for schools in lower-income areas, and in *Maher v. Roe* (1977)[46] and *Harris v. McRae* (1980)[47] it refused to order funding for the procurement of abortions. In the latter two cases, the Court denied that the constitutional right to an abortion required that government pay for it. "It simply does not follow that a woman's freedom of choice carries with it a constitutional entitlement to the financial resources to avail herself of the full range of protected choices." The justices reasoned that it was an indigent woman's poverty, not any law that caused the problem. A decision requiring the funding of abortions would have injected the Supreme Court into the policy question of how public welfare monies should be spent, a matter wholly legislative in character. The Court reasoned similarly in the *Rodriguez* case, in which the plaintiffs had demanded that the Court overrule property tax programs that frequently yielded less funds for lower than for higher-income area schools.

Unfortunately, the Court did not subsequently always maintain its restraint. *Plyler v. Doe*[48] (1982) presented the question whether Texas could deny to the children of illegal aliens the free public education it provides to the children of citizens of legally admitted aliens. The Court invalidated the Texas law and required the state to fund such education, thus crossing the legislative line it had observed in the school tax and abortion cases. Restraint returned several years later with *Kadrmas v. Dickinson*[49] (1988) which decided that a North Dakota statute allowing some public school districts to charge parents for bus transportation was constitutional, with the justices refusing to require the state to spend for this purpose.

Judges and commentators who support judicially mandated spending programs insist that such programs are essential to remedy social ills afflicting certain portions of the population. In doing so, they tend to ignore the full societal implications of those decisions that may make them more harmful than helpful. In *Plyler,* the Court-mandated funding will be acquired, as in *Shapiro,* from other programs or from the taxpayers. In making its decision, the Court did not investigate the importance of existing programs that might, as a result, have to be limited. Nor did it consider the effect of increased taxes on individuals and corporations and on the economic welfare of the state or community. The Court made its decision upon one basis alone—the perceived impact upon certain children of denying them free education—which is but a single facet of a complex problem.

In the absence of a more exhaustive probe of costs and benefits, the Court is not in a position to find that the refusal of Texas to supply additional schooling is unjustified. Viewing the problem in light of the state's many educational and financial concerns is far different from considering the problem by itself, and thus could yield an entirely different answer. In any event, the inquiry required is far too vast and uncertain to be judicially manageable; yet any determination significantly short of it is unsatisfactory and unsound—it simply does not provide a credible base for overruling a legislature. This is added reason for resolving these matters at the legislative, not the judicial, level.

The separation principle involved in each of these cases should be the decisive issue. As expressed in an 1880 decision, the Supreme Court "cannot take upon itself to supply the defects and omissions of state legislation. It would ill perform the duties assigned to it by assuming power properly belonging to the legislative department of the state."[50] This concern is further discussed later in this book in chapter 7 defining and comparing liberties and entitlements.

## III  Protection of Liberty

Most of the rights protected in the United States Constitution are set forth in the Bill of Rights, which consists of the first ten amendments ratified in 1791, about three years after ratification of the original Constitution in 1788. Since it did not contain a bill of rights, the original Constitution was not very informative about the safeguards it accorded the people. While some liberties were secured specifically, most were protected indirectly, by the fact that the Constitution established a government of limited and enumerated powers. As far as the federal constitution was concerned, people were free to engage in activity that the federal government was not empowered to restrict. For many in that period, this kind of protection was unsatisfactory and they sought specific protections by way of a bill of rights.

In the debates in the individual states on ratification of the Constitution, the Federalists (proponents of the proposed Constitution) strongly defended their decision to omit a bill of rights. They contended that the national government was so limited in power that a bill of rights was unnecessary; moreover, an enumeration of specific rights might be harmful since first, it would imply the existence of power where there was none, and, second, it might not list all rights that were protected, to the detriment of those omitted. Arguing that such a bill was unnecessary, Alexander Hamilton asserted that people's rights would be fully preserved by the Supreme Court which had the power to declare void laws exceeding their makers' Constitutional authority.[51]

As a matter of theory, the Federalists were correct that the federal government did not have power to deprive the people of their liberties except where specifically authorized to do so. The Bill of Rights mostly secures rights that were already protected under the common law and which the Federalists maintained would not be diminished by the adoption of the Constitution.

The problem with omitting specific protections such as those contained in the Bill is that in their absence the Supreme Court may not give sufficient recognition to them. In its decisions concerning omitted rights, the court's reasoning would concern primarily the reach of governmental powers, and might not give adequate protection to individual interests. A plaintiff would seem to be in a much stronger position to assert a denial of a specific guarantee when it is listed rather than absent in the Constitution. The Bill of Rights met Federalists' concerns about the omission of some rights by including the Ninth Amendment which states that the "enumeration in the Constitution of certain rights shall not be construed to deny or disparage others retained by the peoples."[52] This provision recognized the existence of unenumerated rights and gave legitimacy to their enforcement.

As previously discussed, not only was the original Constitution devoid of many specific protections, it also failed to provide guidelines on interpretation. The political parties viewed the Constitution differently. Federalists considered the text as providing for an expansive view of federal power, while Republicans believed in a narrow reading of these powers. This difference in interpretation was enough to decide many controversies.

Although the ratification of a bill of rights augmented the legal balance for aggrieved parties, it did little to define the area that was protected. As with the body of the Constitution, the Bill of Rights also employs crisp language that does not give specific information about the scope of its guarantees. The Bill may have narrowed the court's discretion, but this discretion continued to be extensive in interpreting the scope and extent of government powers as well as in construing the meaning of the various enumerated rights and in securing and defining unenumerated rights.

The principal limitation on this discretion was the common law. William Blackstone, the great English commentator of the Eighteenth Century, explained the limits of both governmental authority and individual autonomy in this famous passage:

> [Civil liberty] is no other than natural liberty so far restrained by human laws (and no farther) as is necessary and expedient for the general advantage of the public. Hence we may collect that the law, which restrains a man from doing mischief to his fellow citizens, though it diminishes the natural, increases the civil liberty of mankind: but every wanton and causeless restraint of the will of the subject, whether practiced by a monarch, a nobility, or a popular assembly, is a degree of tyranny. Nay, that even laws themselves, whether made with or without our consent, if they regulate and constrain our conduct in matters of mere indifference, without any good end in view, are laws destructive of liberty.... [T]hat constitution or frame of government, that system of laws, is alone calculated to maintain civil liberty, which leaves the subject entire master of his own conduct, except in those points wherein the public good requires some direction or restraint.[53]

For Blackstone, a law that restrains liberty is acceptable only when it furthers the public good. This is the theme of all rights jurisprudence, and it requires intensive probing of both the person's and the state's interests. In American constitutional adjudication, this analysis takes the form of tests to determine whether the legislative means substantially achieves the legislative ends; whether the means and ends are legitimate; and whether when restraint is necessary, the one utilized is the least onerous option. Thus, Chief Justice Marshall declared that for legislation to be constitutional, the end has to be legitimate, and the means appropriate and plainly adapted to that end.[54]

Experience has shown that this common law approach has guided and restrained the judges in both the United States and other common law countries.[55] It is probably also applicable elsewhere in the western world. To the best of my knowledge, Blackstone's guides on determining validity of legislative restraints on liberty are not codified in any constitution. Within their authority, courts apply them as they deem best or appropriate. Before discussing this concern in greater detail, let us consider the contemporary constitutional experience of Czechoslovakia and Bulgaria, former communist countries that have adopted new constitutional documents. I have also included a discussion of constitution drafting in Ukraine. These documents suffer from the same problem affecting the United States Constitution, the absence of linkage between powers and protections. Aggravating the problem is loose draftsmanship, a matter harmful to all legal instruments, and especially to documents affecting entire nations. We begin this discussion with a consideration of communist constitutions.

## IV Communist Constitutions

As is to be expected, constitutions in communist countries differ considerably from those in the Western democracies that partially or entirely separate the powers of government. The communist constitutions set forth in considerable detail the powers of government and the rights of the people. While they may specifically protect private ownership, freedom of speech and press, and many other freedoms, they do so conditionally and without judicial review. Most important, the legislature is supreme under these constitutions, and since they are the products of a peculiar kind of process granting special consideration to the Communist Party, individual rights in the Western sense are virtually non-existent.

While the constitution of the Union of Socialist Republics adopted in 1977 guarantees major liberties, Article 39 states "Enjoyment by citizens of their rights and freedoms must not be to the detriment of the interests of society or the state, or infringe the rights of other citizens." Similarly, the former communist constitution of Bulgaria[56] guarantees the major liberties, but also provides (Article 9): "Rights and liberties cannot be exercised to the detriment of the public interest." Whatever uncertainty remains under this provision is totally dispelled by the powers given the legislature in Article 85 as follows:

(1) The National Assembly sees to it that the laws do not run counter to the Constitution.

(2) It alone decides whether a law runs counter to the Constitution and whether the conditions for its issue required by the Constitution have been observed.

Under this constitution, the Bulgarian National Assembly is the final arbiter of liberty. To be sure, in the absence of a written Constitution in that nation, the English Parliament has the same powers but the English tradition prohibits its exercise to the detriment of individual liberties. And, of course, England has no Communist Party officially monitoring the government. In the words of Justice Bradley, England's unwritten constitution rests in the understanding that its violation in any material respect "would produce a revolution in an hour."[57] The English orientation toward personal liberties is almost directly opposite that of the communists. While Parliament is supreme, the English courts have protected liberties in their interpretation of statutes, administrative regulations and the common law. Nonetheless, there has been considerable sentiment in England for the adoption of a written bill of rights to provide increased personal protections.

## V  The New Czech and Slovac Charter

The Eastern European nations have been engaged in constitution writing, and some early results are not encouraging from the perspective of the individual. Protections in the "Charter of Fundamental Rights and Freedoms" adopted January 9, 1991 by the Czech and Slovak Federal Republic are conditional, seemingly more on the order of a communist than of the United States Constitution. Thus, privacy, property, movement, religious liberty, expression, assembly and other activities are protected but conditionally:

1. Privacy "may be limited only in cases specified by law." Art. 7(1).

2. Property "may not be misused to the detriment of the rights of others or against legally protected public interests. Its exercise may not cause damage to human health, nature and the environment beyond statutory limits." Art. 11(3).

3. "Sanctity of the home is inviolable" but may be interfered with by law "only if it is essential in a democratic state for protecting the life or health of individuals, for protecting the rights and freedoms of others, or for averting a serious threat to public security and order." Art. 12(3).

4. Freedom of movement is guaranteed but "may be limited by law if it is essential for the security of the State, for maintenance of public order, for protection of the rights and freedoms of others, and in demarcated areas also for the purpose of protecting nature." Art. 14(3).

5. Freedom of religion "may be limited by the law in the case of measures which are essential in a democratic society for protection of public security and order, health and morality, or the rights and freedoms of others." Art. 16(4).

6. Freedom of expression "may be limited by law in the case of measures essential in a democratic society for protecting the rights and freedoms of others, the security of the State, public security, public health, and morality." Art. 17(4).

7. Right of assembly "may be limited by law in the case of assemblies held in public places, if measures are involved, which are essential in a democratic society for protecting the rights and freedoms of others, public order, health, morality, prosperity, or the security of the State." Art. 19(2).

The exception to the rights are broad and enable a court so disposed to apply them in a manner that might ignore the protection and thereby nullify the guarantee itself. The exceptions seem to consume the guarantee. It may be that the nation has great faith in the responsibility of the legislature toward protecting liberties, but it is the purpose of a bill of rights to restrain the legislature and secure libertarian commitments. Some writers have observed that a provision of the Czech and Slovak charter requires the government to honor "the substance and meaning of those rights and freedoms" and that "limits [on them] may not be misused for purposes other than those for which they were intended."[58] These directions may be helpful in safeguarding liberties but the language of much of the balance of the document provides modest comfort against legislative excesses.

## VI Bulgarian Constitution

Adopted July 12, 1991, the Constitution of the Republic of Bulgaria exhibits similar schizophrenia of language. Consider its provisions on the freedom of religion, property, commerce, speech, and press. According to Article 37(1), "Freedom of conscience, freedom of thought, and choice of religion or religious or atheistic views are inviolable." However, Article 37(2) provides "Freedom of conscience and religion may not be detrimental to national security, public order, public health and morality, or the rights and freedoms of other citizens."

Article 39(1) states: "Everyone has the right to express his opinions and disseminate it in writing or orally, through sounds, images, or by any other means." Nonetheless, Article 39(2) provides "This right may not be used to the detriment of the rights and reputations of others or to call for . . . the incitement of enmity. . . ." While Article 40(1) states "The press and other information media are free and not subject to censorship," Article 40(2) provides "A printed publication or any other information medium may be suppressed or confiscated only through an act of judicial authorities, when good mores are violated . . . ." The same give and take is evident in Article 41(1): "Anyone has the right to seek, obtain, or disseminate information. The exercise of this right may not be detrimental to the rights and good names of other citizens, national security, public order, public health, or morality."

Freedom of movement is guaranteed in Article 35(1) subject to restriction "in order to safeguard national security, public health, or the rights and freedoms of other citizens."

"Private property is inviolable" declares Article 17(3). However, the eminent domain provision (Art. 17(5) states: "Expropriation of property in order to meet state or township needs must be according to law and provided that such need cannot be satisfied in any other way. Suitable compensation must be paid in advance." The term suitable may mean no more than appropriate, fitting, or becoming, and does not assure an owner he will be paid fully for or even near the value of the loss.

According to Article 21: "(1) The land is a basic natural resource and benefits from the special protection of the state and society. (2) Arable land may be used exclusively for agriculture purposes. Changes in its use are permitted only when based on proven need, in accordance with conditions and procedures defined by the law." Further inhibiting private ownership and development is Article 18(1): "The state is the sole owner of all underground resources, the coastal beaches, public roadways, waters, forest, and parks of national significance, natural preserves, and archaeological sites, as defined by law."

"The economy of the Republic of Bulgaria is based on free economic initiative" (Art. 19(1)). Freedom of contract is limited, however. Article 19(2) refers to laws "preventing the abuse of monopoly and disloyal competition, and . . . protecting the consumer." Mothers are granted by the state "paid leave, before and after childbirth, free obstetrical care, easier working conditions and other types of social assistance" (47(2)). "Workers and employees have the right to healthy and safe working conditions, a minimal wage, and remuneration consistent with the work done, as well as rest and leave under the conditions and procedures regulated by law" (Art. 48(5)).

Rights under the Constitution include: "Citizens have the right to social security and social assistance" (Art. 51(1)); "Citizens have the right to health insurance . . . and to free medical services, under the conditions and procedures regulated by law" (52(1)); "The right to education is universal" (53(1)); "the right to develop [one's] own culture, in accordance with his ethnic affiliation" (54(1)); "Citizens have the right to a healthy and favorable environment, consistent with stipulated standards and regulations. They have an obligation to protect the environment" (55). The rights referred to in this paragraph are entitlements and their implementation may inhibit protection of economic liberties (see chapter 7).

Perhaps the provisions of the Constitution posing the greatest threat to liberty are contained in Article 57: "(1) The fundamental rights of citizens are irrevocable; (2) These rights may not be abused and may not be exercised to the detriment of the rights or legitimate interests of others." These provisions would provide considerable support for those seeking to limit the exercise of particular freedoms. The words "abuse," "detriment" and "legitimate interests" are far removed from the idea that a person's liberties should be protected unless the state provides substantial justification for the restraint. The quoted language might prevent a court from guaranteeing the exercise of particular activities when those activities are deemed disadvantageous to particular sectors of the society or community, and such an outcome is often to be expected when people assert their rights.

Article 57 has the potential for tilting the Constitution unduly toward protecting the powers of government. Freedom requires eternal vigilance, as Justice Holmes once warned: "When this seemingly absolute protection [of the property right] is found to be qualified by the police power [of the state], the natural tendency of human nature is to extend the qualifications more and more until at last private property disappears."[59] Constitutional language should reduce, not exacerbate this problem.

In the next chapter I shall propose rules for insertion in constitutions relating to the adjudication of restraints on liberty. Both Bulgaria and Czechoslovakia have adopted constitutional documents, but in both instances sufficient ambiguity exists to enable a constitutional court to apply the rules herein proposed for interpreting those documents.

## VII The Proposed Ukrainian Constitution

Under date of June 10, 1992, the Constitutional Commission of the Parliament of Ukraine submitted to the nation a second draft of its proposed Constitution of Ukraine. In the draft, the degree of protection accorded liberties varies and often does not adequately protect an individual liberty. Four examples illustrate the problem.

Article 28 which secures the free exercise of religion provides that "No one may . . . refuse to obey laws on religious grounds." However, a law may make the practice of a given faith difficult and thereby penalize or impede it. As United States Supreme Court Justice Sandra O'Connor has observed, "laws neutral toward religion can coerce a person to violate his religious conscience or intrude upon his religious duties just as effectively as laws aimed at religion."[60] Laws that burden the exercise of religion should require strong justification by the government.

Article 28 also provides that the "rousing of hostility and hatred on religious grounds shall be punishable under the law." Broad language of this character would justify serious limitations on freedom of expression.

Article 29 states that any abridgement of the right of expression "shall be only for the purposes of protecting individual, family, professional, commercial or state secrets, assuring state and civil security, territorial integrity, respect of other citizens' rights and freedoms, and protecting people's health and civil morality." This language gives the legislature great discretion to limit freedom of speech.

Article 14 (part two) provides: "The constitutional rights of citizens may not be restricted except in the interest of protecting the rights and freedoms of other persons, preservation of the general welfare, or in defense of state or social security, health and morality." The words are so broad as to minimize the protection afforded any constitutional guarantee.

Various provisions are ambiguous in the protection they afford ownership and investment. "No one may be arbitrarily deprived of his or her property." (Art. 36). The word "arbitrarily" gives the interpreter great discretion in defining it, thereby reducing the certainty of the property guarantee.

"The exercise of the right of ownership must not contradict the interests of society as a whole and the rights of individual natural persons and legal entities." (Art. 36). Again, the definitions of critical words in this provision can vary enormously, and therefore an owner's protection is not secure.

"The right of private property to land shall be acquired on grounds and within limits established by the law. . . . With the purpose of ensuring rational and ecologically safe use of land and establishing just social relations, the law shall impose certain duties on the landowner [and] set maximum limits on private ownership. . . ." (Art. 68). This language grants the government great powers to restrict the ownership and use of property.

"Restriction on freedom of entrepreneurship, agreements and competition shall be allowed only in such cases and in such a manner specified by law, as stipulated in part two of Article 14 [previously quoted herein] of this constitution." (Art. 74). After reading these two provisions, a prospective investor might well be concerned that there is little protection for a business against confiscation.

Interestingly, under its law on foreign investment of April 1992, Ukraine protects economic liberties. Articles 9 and 10 guarantee foreign investors against adverse changes in legislation and against expropriations and unlawful acts of government bodies and officials. Article 11 provides for compensation and damages for losses incurred by foreign investors as a result of improper governmental acts and omissions.[61] Such protections among others should be established under the constitution and mostly would be included in the relevant language contained in Article VI of the suggested model constitution that appears in Appendix I hereof. Because it is much more difficult to amend than a statute, a constitutional guarantee is the strongest form of legal protection, one which prospective investors are entitled to expect.

The proposed Ukraine constitution mandates a lavish program of awards and benefits as protected rights including:

Rest, leisure, paid vacations, "fair" and "satisfactory" wages, and other welfare benefits for workers; minimum wages and living standards; equal pay for the same amount of work in accordance with its quality and quantity; free medical service; safe environment and foodstuffs; free education (including professional education); housing; and a reduced work period for mothers with young children, minors, and people with limited ability to work.

If the Ukraine economy is a poor one, how will it provide for the host of benefits the proposed constitution seeks to bestow? If the entitlements are satisfied, how much will be left to pay for police and fire protection, military security, government administration, and the installation of streets, sewers and water mains? A nation must also limit the tax burden lest it destroy the economy.

The proposed constitution would thus be imposing great restraints on the private sector as well as on the political process. For the reasons set forth in this book, these mandates are not consistent with contemporary aspirations for freedom and abundance.

# 5
# Judicial Rules for the Protection of Liberty

In a governmental system where the powers of government are separate, the role of the judiciary is to interpret the constitution and declare unconstitutional laws that violate it. Among the most difficult of interpretative problems—yet among the most important—is to determine when the legislature or executive has deprived people of their liberties. This issue is at the basis of modern constitutional thought, that majorities are supreme except when they limit rights of minorities. In limiting liberty, when is the legislature or executive acting within its powers and when in excess of them?

Constitutions rarely provide specific answers in this area. Nevertheless this conflict between authority and liberty continually demands solutions. The problem is three-fold: First, constitutions are composites of powers and guarantees, each separately stated without linkage or priority to other provisions. Second, all such provisions are usually set forth in very broad language. Third, while interpretation must involve some application of personal value choices, such subjectivity should be minimized. The critical responsibility of interpretation must not rest on personal beliefs of judges; the rule of law is expected to protect us from such arbitrary power. The constitutional decision should be principled, "one that rests on reasons with respect to all issues in the case, reasons that in their generality and their neutrality transcend any immediate result that is involved."[62]

Constitutional interpretation is generally more difficult than statutory interpretation. Statutes are passed with specific objectives in mind, and cover reasonably well the facts to which they are applied. Inasmuch as constitutions deal with principles which are not necessarily directed at immediate concerns, the relationship between constitutional language and specific events is usually more remote. When the conflict between authority and liberty is involved, a constitutional court may often depart from strict application of either and engage in balancing the interests between the two. The problem with balancing is that it opens the decision making process to the interpreter's personal values and beliefs. Statutory interpretation is also subject to some balancing but to a far lesser degree.

Framers of new constitutions for nations formerly subject to communist rule confront the dual problem of establishing a viable and effective government and at the same time maximizing individual liberty. In interpreting the United States Constitution, the United States Supreme Court seems to have dealt reasonably well with this problem; at least the nation has experienced major domestic and foreign crises and generally preserved a great measure of liberty. However, the constitutional text itself does not provide much guidance in resolving the tension between authority and liberty; this is a failing of the United States Constitution that should be avoided by modern constitution writers.

Different parts of the U.S. Constitution deal separately with authority and liberty, and there is little language explaining or defining the relationship. Containing only about twenty book-size pages, the document employs brief, eloquent sentences and clauses that deal summarily both with very important government powers and critical personal guarantees, with little or no linkage between them. Thus, most provisions of the Bill of Rights are set forth in absolute terms, yet they are not intended to be absolute. The Constitution grants Congress numerous powers and a necessary and proper power to implement them; yet the exercise of any power must at times be subordinate to the preservation of individual rights.[63]

The ultimate source of constitutional meaning should be the text and not the interpreters. Inasmuch as the language of the United States Constitution does not reveal the breadth of protection for any right, the Supreme Court may greatly enlarge or restrict it. Experience discloses the range of discretion the Court has exercised in securing liberties. The Court has given maximum protection to freedom of speech and press, an intermediate level of protection to property rights, and minimum protection to economic rights. No language in the Constitution authorizes or in any manner provides for this hierarchy. It is entirely a product of judicial interpretation.

Next to the bill of rights, Section 1 of the fourteenth amendment is the principal source of individual guarantees in the United States Constitution. It provides as follows:

> No state shall make or enforce any law which shall abridge the privileges or immunities of citizens of the United States; nor shall any state deprive any person of life, liberty, or property, without due process of law; nor

deny to any person within its jurisdiction the equal protection of the laws.[64]

The protections thus provided are very broad and far less specific than in the Bill of Rights, again enabling the Supreme Court to exercise great prerogative in interpretation. The Thirty-Ninth Congress, which framed this section, intended each clause to curtail considerably the powers of the states. The judicial decisions are not consistent with this objective. For all practical purposes, the United States Supreme Court has excised the privileges and immunities clause from the Constitution while giving very broad scope to the due process and equal protection clauses.

Interestingly, decided just 3 years after ratification of the amendment, the *Slaughter-House Cases*[65] by a 5–4 vote construed Section 1 in a manner that, according to one authoritative commentator, "ignore[d] virtually every word said in the debates" of the 39th Congress that framed it.[66] In time, however, the Court interpreted the due process and equal protection clauses to provide numerous protections against state action.

Justices of the United States Supreme Court continually claim commitment to the rule of law in their decisions and not to personal goals and values. In their efforts to achieve objectivity, the Justices have created and applied over the years numerous tests to determine whether a constitutional violation has occurred. When deprivation of liberties is alleged, the Court has frequently utilized a Blackstonian perspective[67] to decide if the federal or state government has sufficient justification for its restraint. Jurists in other nations have also followed this course.

This kind of approach to interpretation should specifically be prescribed by a constitution and not left to the uncertainties of judicial wisdom. In writing constitutions, framers should use language securing each liberty without qualification or reservation. However, the constitution should state that no liberties are absolute, and should set forth a constitutional formula (as explained subsequently) to be applied by the judiciary to determine if a particular governmental restraint justifies a limitation on liberty.

Under a separation of powers system, each branch of government must prove authority for its actions. When an act of either the legislature or the executive is challenged as violating individual rights, the burden should be on the government to justify the restraint. When liberties are in question, the government discretion as to means is confined to essential restraints and does not include capricious or unnecessary ones. To limit liberty arbitrarily or without purpose is the epitome of oppression.

At a minimum, the government should prove that the purpose of the law is constitutionally authorized, that it will be achieved by this law, that the law will not have a disproportionate or capricious impact on liberty (Blackstone's "wanton and causeless restraint"),[68] and that the same purpose cannot be achieved with a law less harmful to liberty. More formally, a constitutional court adjudicating challenges to governmental authority should require that the government prove the existence of each of the following four conditions.

*First, the objective of the law or regulation is within the power of the government body that adopted it.*

This means that (1) in adopting the restraint the government has complied with all constitutionally required procedures, and (2) the law seeks to advance a legitimate legislative purpose. The rule merely makes certain the government is acting within the scope of its authority.

Legislators always maintain their objective is to promote the common good even when in fact it is not. For the review to be meaningful, the judiciary should not be bound by stated intentions and should seek to determine the actual purpose. This requires delving beyond the stated purposes and post hoc rationalizations into the history and political circumstances attending the enactment to ascertain what the lawmakers sought to achieve.

The court should go no further than to decide legitimacy of purpose. American and Canadian courts may require in addition that the objective be "important," a rule that according to Chief Justice Rehnquist is "so diaphanous and elastic as to invite subjective judicial preferences or prejudices relating to particular types of legislation."[69]

The requirement that the objective be lawful is a major restraint on the legislature. Prohibiting a right for no other reason than antagonism toward it is deprivation of the right for its own sake—and not a legitimate legislative purpose. Likewise, legislation seeking largely to advance the interests of a private person or group at the expense of individual rights cannot be regarded as advancing a legitimate legislative purpose. Many constitutions provide this protection, but in the absence of such a provision, it should be regarded as inherent in a constitution. Government has a fundamental obligation to govern impartially. It must not deprive one person of liberty solely for the benefit of another person. In a democratic society, only a purpose intended to benefit or protect the public would allow restraint of people.[70]

*Second, the restraint in question is within the power of the government body that adopted it and will substantially achieve its objective; that is, the means is legitimate and the fit between it and the ends is close.*

The means must be no less legitimate than the ends; a legitimate purpose cannot be achieved by an illegitimate law.[71] Laws that do not substantially advance their intended purpose are needless restraints on the people's liberties, and consequently without constitutional merit. In the words of a United States Supreme Court Justice: "If a statute to prevent conflagrations would require householders to pour oil on their roofs as a means of curbing the spread of fire when discovered in the neighborhood, we could hardly uphold it."[72]

In the United States, the means test best known and often applied by the judiciary is referred to as the "clear and present danger" test and concerns limitations on expression. "The question in every case is whether the words used are used in such circumstances and are of such a nature as to create a clear and present danger that they will bring about the substantial evils that Congress has a right to prevent."[73] Thus, a law forbidding speech that will not cause or intensify a particular problem that the legislature seeks to remedy needlessly restricts freedom of expression.

*Third, there is proportionality between the effects of the restraint and its objective; that is, the adverse consequences of the restraint are not out of proportion to its benefits.*

The impact of the limitation upon freedom should not be out of proportion to the objective sought to be achieved. The more severe the deleterious effects of a measure, the more societally important the objective must be. This analysis should include a determination whether the legislation is overinclusive or underinclusive. It should be neither overinclusive—too broad in its impact on people—nor underinclusive—not broad enough to reach substantially the various persons or actions causing the problem.

*Fourth, the same objective cannot be achieved by a law less harmful to the exercise of liberty; that is, no less onerous and feasible alternative legislative solution exists.*

Under this analysis, the court should determine whether the passage of the law imposes restraint more extensive than necessary to achieve the objective intended. The law should impair as little as possible the freedom of concern, and therefore should be precise and narrow. When the application of another more moderate law will achieve a similar result, the government has selected a means that needlessly restricts liberty. Thus, a regulatory law will generally be far less arduous to liberty than a prohibitory law. Regulation is to be preferred over prohibition when each yields similar benefits.

If the government proves each of the foregoing four conditions, the court should sustain the law at issue. Otherwise the law violates protected constitutional liberty and should be nullified. To support a law or regulation under the foregoing inquiry, the government must in effect prove that its enactment is necessary to and will preserve life, liberty or property, broadly defined. This multi-pronged inquiry limits judicial subjectivity by dividing the analysis into relevant parts, rather than deciding it as a whole, without a detailed examination. A detailed explanation will also provide greater guidance in the future for both legislators and judges.

The advantage of a textual basis for this judicial inquiry is disclosed by the Canadian experience. Section 1 of the Canadian Charter of Rights and Freedoms "guarantees the rights and freedoms set out in it subject only to such reasonable limits prescribed by law as can be demonstrably justified in a free and democratic society." The Canadian judiciary has wrestled with this language in attempting to interpret the Charter and has applied much of the preceding four-prong formula in adjudicating the validity of government limitations placed on individual rights. While these efforts have provided a judicial framework, it would seem preferable for such a framework to be established by the constitutional text, particularly in nations without a common law background and tradition. Moreover, such constitutional provisions would provide more certainty about the scope and nature of the inquiry for the judicial interpreters.[74]

The foregoing suggested judicial analysis is premised on the proposition that liberty is not absolute and must yield at times to the authority of the state. The responsibility for justifying a limit on liberty rests with the government entity seeking the limit. This burden should be of intermediate character; the state should not be given either maximum or minimum deference, as is the case in the United States when courts apply either strict or minimal scrutiny to laws limiting the exercise of individual rights. The appropriate standard is the one applied by Canadian courts which hold that the onus of proof justifying a restraint on liberty is on the government, and the standard under its constitution is the ordinary civil standard of proof.[75]

Fairness and equity support the rule requiring the government to carry the burden of proof in these cases. When government proscribes liberties, it has an obligation and responsibility to prove justification for the restraint. The presumption that the state is correct in curtailing people's activities can only be accepted in societies where restraint is normal—those that equate government direction and control with the public interest. Demanding that the aggrieved party assume this obligation operates to limit freedom.[76] As United States Supreme Court Justice McReynolds observed in a New York case involving a law regulating the price of milk: "If necessary for [him] to show absence of the asserted conditions, the little grocer was helpless from the beginning—the practical difficulties were too great for the average man."[77]

In my opinion the United States Supreme Court's application of strict or minimal scrutiny is inconsistent with the idea of separate but similarly powerful branches of government. To subject the legislature's will to a very stringent standard of justification jeopardizes it as a viable branch of government. The judicial branch does not have authority to terminate the political process. While the inquiry should be deep and searching, it must not become "strict in theory and fatal in fact."[78] By the same token, the government should not be given an extreme level of deference in the proof it presents for this would virtually terminate judicial scrutiny.[79] To succeed in proving that a particular restriction on liberty is constitutional, the government must bear the same burden of proof as would be required ordinarily of any plaintiff seeking to establish its case in a court of law.

The preponderance of evidence standard is generally applicable in the United States in civil cases. This standard requires that the trier of fact must be convinced by the party on whom the burden rests, which would be the govrnment in these cases, that a particular fact is more probably true than not true. That is, the evidence produced is more persuasive than that opposed to it, therefore the probability of truth is greater.

The judicial inquiry should also include consideration of the harm caused by an unlawful restraint. A government body or official will have limited incentive to observe individual rights if the sole penalty is invalidation of the law. In addition to striking down the law, the court should impose damages on government fully compensating the injured party for any losses sustained, so that the person or corporation will be at least as well off as before the restriction was applied.

# 6
# Property Rights and Economic Liberties

While the U.S. Supreme Court protects a wide variety of liberties, including ownership of property, it does not guarantee significantly economic liberties, those concerned with the production and distribution of goods and services. This distinction stands out now more than ever as an anomaly in a world where many millions of people have revolted against their government in large measure to secure this liberty.

Government is not more wise or humane when it regulates commerce than when it regulates speech, press or religion. In barring economic freedoms, the communist dictatorships denied people both their human rights and the material abundance that results when individuals exercise freely their talents and abilities in their own self-interest.

The tendency of some constitutional scholars who condemn regulation of expression, religion, and privacy to prefer a strongly regulated economy is remarkable. On an intellectual level, the superiority of freedom over regulation in the economic market has clearly won the lengthy debate. In recent years, six Nobel prizes in economics were awarded to economists who have written that securing economic liberties is essential to the economic viability of the modern state. These scholars are Fredrich Hayek, Milton Friedman, George Stigler, James Buchanan, Ronald Coase and Gary Becker.

The difference in material outcome between free and despotic systems is readily apparent to any observer. Measured by living standards and total output, the economic systems of East Germany, China, and North Korea were disasters compared to those of West Germany, Taiwan, and South Korea. The results are no different when similar comparisons are made everywhere else in the world. Rejection of economic regression and stagnation was a major factor in the people's repudiation of communism.

Studies show the vast differences between economic systems. Thus, Professor Gerald Scully measured the success of open and closed societies and concluded that nations that have chosen to suppress economic, political and civil liberties have gravely reduced the standard of living of their citizens. By contrast material progress is greatest if individuals have the right to pursue their affairs unmolested by the state. According to Scully's studies, politically open societies, which bind themselves to the rule of law, to private property, and to the private allocation of resources grew at three times more (2.73 to 0.91 percent annually) and were two and one half times as efficient as societies where those freedoms were circumscribed or prescribed.[80]

One of the most remarkable economic success stories is that of the city-state of Hong Kong, a sliver of land next to mainland China, whose government exercises minimal controls over the private economic market. It maintains an unusually low level of taxation and regulation. According to economists James Gwartney, Walter Block and Robert Lawson, Hong Kong had the highest measure of economic freedom of any nation in the world for the two periods they studied, 1975 to 1980 and 1985 to 1988. Hong Kong also had annually the world's highest per capita gross national product growth rate for these years. The 1975–1980 annual growth rate was 9.40 percent and the 1985–1988 rate was 8.82 percent.[81]

One of the most densely populated places in the world, this city-state grew from a population of 15,000 in 1841 to over 5,000,000 in 1984. About 98 percent of the population is classified as Chinese on the basis of place of origin and language. It has few natural resources and only one-seventh of the land is arable. The colony is unable to feed itself and almost all industrial materials, capital goods and the vast majority of foodstuffs are imported.

Another city-state with the remarkable economic performance is Singapore which along with Hong Kong has had growth in the gross domestic product per capita of an average of 6 percent per year from 1960 to 1990. Gwartney, Block and Lawson give a lower rating to Singapore than to Hong Kong in their scale of economic freedom. They show for 1975, Hong Kong with a rating of 82.29 and Singapore 60.13; for 1980 the difference is 87.38 to 68.83; 1985, 83.25 to 67.67; and 1988, 82.79 to 73.50. Interestingly, they show that Singapore also has had a lower annual growth per capita gross national product; 6.11 for 1975–80 and 6.35 for 1980–88.[82]

In recent years a number of Latin American countries have instituted free market reforms in their economies with considerable success. The most successful is Chile whose gross domestic product grew by 9.7 percent in 1992, a very impressive level and one of the highest in the world for that year. This was the ninth consecutive year of growth for the nation. Its gross domestic product more than doubled in two decades to $36 billion in 1992. Growth is expected to be in the 6 percent range for 1993. Inflation eased to 12.7 percent in 1992, from 18.7 percent in 1991; the unemployment rate fell to 4.8 percent of the workforce, and investment in 1992 grew by about 20 percent.

A major explanation for these results is the economic reforms that Chile instituted beginning 1975. The nation deregulated many businesses and industries, privatized nearly all state enterprises, eliminated costly subsidies, and allowed market forces to determine interest rates and wages. Monetary controls over exports, imports and foreign investments have been minimized or removed.[83]

The more freedom in the marketplace the more likely it will better provide for the people. Contemporary economic studies show that in the United States, government regulation of economic markets very often operates negatively, the disadvantages outweigh the advantages. The legal restraints on economic activity do more harm than good.

In my book, *Economic Liberties and the Constitution,* I summarized 53 studies of government regulation, by more than 60 individual and institutional researchers, which have appeared in the most prestigious scholarly literature. These studies show that although every regulation accomplishes some purpose, the great majority fail a cost/benefit analysis. Indicative of their conclusions, the vast bulk of these scholars favor either total or substantial deregulation of the area under study.[84]

As revealed in these studies, much regulation has resulted in the reduction of economic efficiency, misallocation of resources, and redistribution of income from the consumer to the regulated group. Considered as a whole, economic regulations seriously limit a nation's productivity and output. A common finding in these studies is that the regulation of concern raises prices, first, by restricting competition, and second, by imposing a variety of unnecessary requirements on producers and sellers that increase cost. People of average and lesser income, those least able to afford higher prices, are the most adversely affected.

As the subsequent pages will disclose, there are many explanations for the failures of regulations. Thus, a proposed restriction may be based on the best intention and information but this does not mean that it will accomplish its purposes. For such proposals to obtain the force of law, the legislative and administrative authorities must adopt necessary statutes and regulations to implement them. However, the record of the political process in this respect has not been very good. The perfect plan is often quite imperfect by the time it emerges from the pressures and compromises of the legislative process, whether it be on a local or higher government level, and it might be ravaged still more as administered. It is possible that the courts may lay some or much of the plan to rest.

Consider the comments on regulation by Professor Ronald Coase, 1991 Nobel Laureate in economics, who was for a long time the editor of the very highly respected *Journal of Law & Economics.* The *Journal* published over the years numerous studies on economic regulation, and Coase concludes:

> The main lesson to be drawn from these studies is clear; they all tend to suggest that the regulation is either ineffective or that, when it has a noticeable impact, on balance the effect is bad, so that consumers obtain a worse product or a higher-priced product or both as a result of the regulation. Indeed, this result is found so uniformly as to create a puzzle; one would expect to find in all these studies at least some government programs that do more good than harm.[85]

Professor Coase believes that, in theory at least, there is no reason why government regulation cannot improve on market processes. He states, however, "My puzzle is to explain why these occasions seem to be so rare, if not non-existent."[86]

The experience of government regulation in the United States reveals the great difficulty of maintaining economic freedoms in democratic societies. Economic regulation emanates chiefly from two different sources. The first source is those people who demand the passage of laws to remedy what they see as problems in the economic system. They are motivated by ideological or more general public interest reasons. Members of this group do not directly benefit from the laws they propose or favor.

This second source of economic regulation is those individuals and corporations who seek regulation in their own self interest. Most of the people in this group are in business, trades, or professions. They want regulations imposed to limit the market usually as a means of obtaining more income for themselves.

The second group is engaged in rent seeking, a term used by economists to identify actions by individuals and interest groups intended to change public policy with respect to taxes, spending and regulation in a manner that will redistribute more income to themselves. In addition to obstructing the market, rent seeking requires the employment of lawyers and lobbyists in activities that do not advance productive activity.[87]

The second group accounts for a great deal of regulation—perhaps most of it. In a democratic society, legislators are highly receptive to the demands of their constituents. As a result, a relatively small number of persons seeking to obtain monetary gains have considerable political opportunity to do so. Judge Richard Posner has suggested that the lawmaking process creates a market for legislation in which politicians "sell" legislative protection to those who could help their electoral prospects with money or votes or both.[88]

Professor Michael Granfield has likened the legislature to a general store whose inventory includes monopolies, preferences, and concessions. The politicians sells these goods, as any astute store owner would, to the group offering the highest price. The arrangement does not necessarily include bribery or any other illegal activity. It may simply involve a legal contribution or a promise of votes.[89]

The process that leads to legislation benefitting comparatively few people is not difficult to understand. Those who would be helped monetarily by laws have the incentive to wage a strong lobbying effort, whereas those who would bear the cost without sharing the benefits frequently do not have sufficient personal stake to fight for their position. The concentration of benefits provides a special interest group with an incentive for creating a narrow political lobby, whose small size makes organizing relatively easy.

On the other side, a larger number of citizens are involved; they are often widely dispersed and frequently have little or no knowledge of the proposed laws or the probable effects. Further, the costs of the legislation are spread so that few persons suffer very much, which limits incentive to organize. As a consequence, the costs of spending measures, subsidies, and special economic preferences are passed along, often to an unknowing and uncomplaining public.

Yet, considered as a whole, many studies disclose that regulation in the United States is very costly. A recent study estimates that federal regulation may be costing American taxpayers $400–500 billion annually over those costs of government disclosed in the national budget. This amounts to an average of $4000 to $5000 per household.[90]

These figures do not separate what might be termed "necessary" and "unnecessary" regulations. Even assuming a considerable amount of these costs is for "necessary" regulations, experience in this area reveals that a huge portion is being spent as a result of government controls that do not protect or benefit people's lives and property. It should also be noted that perhaps the most expensive of "unnecessary" controls are those which operate to inhibit the human skills that advance society. The emerging nations have suffered greatly from this problem. Because of less regulations, the number and variety of products and services are much more plentiful in capitalist than in communist nations.

Given the incentives of the political process, the well being of property owners and entrepreneurs can be precarious. Reform groups who reject or distrust market mechanisms, and various interests who seek monetary gain, have considerable opportunity to achieve their goals, particularly when they have common aims, as they often do.

The protection of owners and entrepreneurs from the power and might of these special economic interests demands both insertion of economic guarantees in a constitution and the existence of a judiciary with the power to enforce them.

# I   Provisions on Condemnation and Regulation
## The United States Experience

In my talks with leaders of emerging states, I concluded that many do not understand the high level of protection accorded property ownership in the democratic nations. To provide such knowledge, this section contains information on recent legal decisions in the United States in the area of land use regulations. This information also should be most useful to constitution drafters.

In a free society, government should not be the final arbiter of property use. This is clearly the intent of the "takings" clause of the United States Constitution which states as part of the Fifth Amendment that "private property shall [not] be taken for public use without just compensation." Yet, for a long time, specifically from about the mid-1920s to the early 1980s, the U.S. Supreme Court frequently sustained quite severe land use regulation. Beginning in 1987, the U.S. Supreme Court has changed policy and shown a much stronger disposition to protect property rights.

Three cases reveal this trend. *First English Lutheran Church of Glendale v. County of Los Angeles,*[91] decided in 1987, held that landowners are entitled to just compensation when an ordinance temporarily or permanently denies them all use of their land. *Nollan v. California Coastal Commission,*[92] also decided in 1987, ruled that, for a land use regulation to be valid it must substantially advance a legitimate state interest. The court held invalid a California Coastal Commission requirement that the land owners dedicate a public easement across their land on the basis that the easement would not achieve the stated public purpose.

The most recent case is *Lucas v. South Carolina Coastal Council*[93] (1992) which involved two oceanfront lots purchased by Mr. Lucas for about one million dollars. At the time of the purchase, the applicable laws allowed the lots to be used for construction of housing. After Lucas bought the land, South Carolina adopted a law prohibiting the construction of any habitable structures in the area where the land was located. The United States Supreme Court held that unless nuisance laws in existence at the time of Lucas' purchase prohibited construction of the houses, the state had unconstitutionally deprived him of the property.

All of these decisions place a burden on land use regulators to provide considerable justification for their rules. The opinions are consistent with the general long-existing principle that the use of land is constitutionally secured so long as the use is not harmful. What is meant by harm? In a society whose economy is based on ownership and investment, the term should be defined to preserve the productivity, creativity and ingenuity of the private sector. Pursuant to this principle, regulation that truly secures public health and safety and forbids noxious uses would be considered legitimate.

The standard for determining validity required by the *Nollan* case embodies two tests: first, whether in adopting a land use regulation the government is seeking to achieve a legitimate state interest; and second, whether the regulation substantially effectuates this interest. Both tests are common in rights jurisprudence litigation, in which a court seeks to determine if a particular regulation violates a person's constitutional rights.

In the *Nollan* case, the Supreme Court determined that the regulation failed the second test of the standard. It struck down the California Coastal Commission's requirement that the Nollans convey to the public an easement paralleling the ocean coast which the land adjoined, as a condition of obtaining a demolition permit for an existing bungalow they planned to replace with a new house. The court reasoned that such an easement did not substantially advance the alleged state interest of making the ocean both visually and "psychologically" accessible to the public.

In a footnote in *Nollan,* the Court discussed but did not decide the issue of disproportionate impact raised in the case. The Commission claimed that allowing the Nollans to build their house without dedicating the easement would result in a row of homes between the ocean and the road on the other side of the property that would prevent travellers on the road from being aware of the proximity of the ocean. The court replied that if the Nollans were being singled out to bear the burden of California's attempt to remedy this problem even though they had not contributed to it more than other coastal landowners, the state action—even if otherwise valid—might violate the takings clause or the equal protection clause of the Constitution. "One of the principal purposes of the takings clause is to 'bar government from forcing some people alone to bear public burdens which, in all fairness and justice, should be born by the public as a whole.'"[94]

The court's observations are relevant to ordinances that limit or tax new development because of the alleged inadequacies of existing facilities or services. Thus, congested roads may become more congested with the arrival of newcomers, but the problem is not solely attributable to newcomers; rather, it is due to the development of the entire locality. If the community had not developed so extensively, the newcomers' impact would not be significant.

In *Lucas* the court said that there were at least two discreet categories of government action that required compensation without any case-specific inquiry whether the public interest was advanced by the restraint. The first encompasses regulations that compel the property owner to suffer a physical "invasion" of his property. In general, no matter how minute the intrusion, no matter how weighty the public purpose behind it, the court has required compensation. For example, the court held in an earlier case that New York's law requiring landlords to allow television cable companies to install cable facilities in their apartment buildings constituted a taking of property, even though the facility occupied at most only one and one-half cubic feet of the landlord's property.[95]

The second situation in which the court has found a categorical treatment appropriate is where the regulation denies an owner all economically beneficial or productive use of the land. South Carolina contended it acted, among other reasons, to prevent the erosion and destruction of the state's beach and dune area which would be brought about by the kind of development Lucas planned for his two lots. It also said it was in the state's best interest to protect and promote beach access for local residents and tourists. The South Carolina Supreme Court accepted the state's reasoning as justifying the regulation and reversed the lower court which found the law to be a taking of property.

The United States Supreme Court stated that when a person buys property, he obtains absolute protection against a regulatory denial of all economically beneficial or productive use, subject to the legal restraints such as nuisance laws then restricting the use of the property. The court viewed South Carolina's assertion of harm as much too broad and consequently a deprivation of the owner's rights. The legislature is limited to applying nuisance laws that were in existence at the time of the land's acquisition. In imposing these nuisance laws, the state does not deprive the owner of any rights since the interest acquired was subject to these laws.

Thus, the harm that would justify South Carolina's prohibitions on the Lucas property are those that do no more than duplicate the result that could have been achieved in the courts, either by adjacent landowners or other uniquely affected persons under the state's law of private nuisance, or by the state under its power to abate nuisances. The United States Supreme Court returned the case to the South Carolina courts for reconsideration pursuant to the standards it set forth.

Under the common law in the United States, there are both public and private nuisances. A public nuisance is an interference with a right common to the general public such as living under the conditions of health and safety and distant from structures used for noxious or immoral activities. A private nuisance is an unreasonable interference with an owner's use and enjoyment of the property. To be regarded as a nuisance, the activity must result in substantial and unreasonable harm to the owner's said interests. Nuisance is distinguishable from trespass which is an interference with an owner's right to exclusive possession of the land. Thus noise, smells, threats of harm and vibrations are characteristics of nuisance, while physical invasion by dust and rocks would be a trespass.

In private nuisance cases, once it is decided that the interference is substantial, the question is whether the complaining owner should be required to bear it without compensation. One factor entering into this analysis is whether the harm to the owner outweighs the utility of the conduct in question. The purpose of nuisance law is to secure property rights by terminating injurious and noxious uses that destroy property rights.[96]

Of particular interest in the *Lucas* case is the reasoning of the court that the second categorical standard may be violated by a deprivation of what it has termed, "an owner's reasonable investment-backed expectations." In these circumstances, the issue is whether the government has deprived an owner of a valuable interest he purchased.

Owners should not be denied a use they contracted for or be forced to devote their properties to a use which, albeit it one which might benefit the government's best interests, bears no relation to any economic purpose which could be reasonably contemplated by a private investor. If a regulation deprives an owner of the distinct objectives of ownership, it has deprived him of his reasonable investment-backed expectations. A market economy operates on the understanding that an investor's expectations will be legally protected. The taking clause "protects private expectations to ensure private investment."[97] As Blackstone has stated, "the public good is in nothing more essentially interested, than the protection of every individual's private rights."[98]

Accordingly, an owner's reasonable investment-backed expectations may involve a portion of the property that is less than the whole. As a general proposition, a total deprivation of an owner's interest is not required for a taking to occur: the abrogation of a legally distinguishable property interest is sufficient. Such interest may be of various kinds. Protected property interests comprehend "every sort of interest the citizen may possess."[99] Compensation would be required solely for the part of the property that is taken.

Nor should government escape liability when it only takes a portion of the property. As the United States Supreme Court has stated:

> It would be a very curious and unsatisfactory result, if. . .it shall be held that if the government refrains from the absolute conversion of real property to the uses of the public it can destroy its value entirely, can inflict irreparable and permanent injury to any extent, can, in effect, subject it to total destruction without making any compensation, because, in the narrowest sense of the word, it is not *taken* for the public use.[100]

Hence, according to the New York Court of Appeals in a 1989 decision, a taking may occur without reference to monetary loss. A New York City ordinance prohibited the demolition, alteration, or conversion of single-room occupancy (SRO) properties and obligated the owners to restore all units to habitable condition and lease them at controlled rents for an indefinite period. The City contended that the law was an effort to help reduce the severe problems of homelessness by preserving the stock of low-rent SRO housing. The Court held the ordinance invalid as both a physical and regulatory taking in violation of the federal and State constitutions.[101] It found that the ordinance "abrogates or substantially impairs" each of the owners' basic rights to possess, use and dispose of their buildings.[102]

In *First English*, the County of Los Angeles argued that to increase the risk that a taking would be found and government required to pay for it would chill the planning and regulatory process. The Supreme Court agreed, but asserted that

> such consequences necessarily flow from any decision upholding a claim for constitutional rights; many of the provisions of the constitution are designed to limit the flexibility and freedom of governmental authorities and the just compensation clause of the fifth amendment is one of them. As Justice Holmes aptly noted more than 50 years ago, "A strong public desire to improve the public condition is not enough to warrant achieving the desire by a shorter cut than the constitutional way of paying for the change."[103]

## Limiting the Legislature

Among others, a contemporary constitution should secure the rights of religion, speech, press, research, teaching, assembly, petition, association, movement, ownership, and investment. As previously explained, protected rights must not be limited in the absence of a constitutional justification for such restraint.

Generally, contemporary constitutions do not provide sufficient protection for the liberties of property and enterprise. The nations emerging into freedom do not have the option of following this practice. Their economic viability necessitates attracting foreign and domestic investment, which will be difficult to accomplish unless ownership and entrepreneurship are legally secured.

These nations confront the problem of changing their economic system from one dominated by central planning to one emphasizing private markets. A market system is based on ownership and development by private individuals and corporations of the means of production and distribution. This system must function mainly on its own, separated and insulated from the government. Potential owners and entrepreneurs must feel secure that they can participate in it without fear of confiscation, repression or economic instability. Accordingly, the system requires a legal framework that will safeguard its objectives and operations.

In the past, communist governments have allowed foreign firms to operate within their countries but mostly on the basis of individual contracts between the government and the firm. Such agreements are inconsistent with a private economic system. They enable the government—not the market—to determine the firms that will be permitted entry and the terms under which they will operate. Market economies function differently: the marketplace should control the existence and character of an enterprise. Potential owners and entrepreneurs should be able to engage in activities of their choice without securing official "blessing."

A market economy requires strong but not absolute legal protection against government controls. In a market economy, there are only three ways in which the state can obtain private property or property rights from people in the absence of their consent: *condemnation, regulation,* and *taxation.* These powers are essential to the operation of government, but they should be used sparingly if the market is to function efficiently and effectively.

Investors generally understand that the power of *condemnation* is inherent in government and accept this principle provided the state applies it in accordance with internationally recognized limitations such as those set forth in the United States Constitution: Private property shall not be taken for public use without just compensation.[104]

There are four operative words in this guarantee. To assure investor confidence and secure individual rights, each should be defined from the perspective of promoting a free economy. The objective should be to maximize an owner's protections against confiscation, yet enable government to obtain property required to conduct essential services. I submit the following definitions:

*Private property* includes any asset or thing of value owned by a private person or corporation; *taken* means (1) the government obtaining full or partial ownership, possession or control of private property, or (2) the government damaging private property and thereby destroying its value in whole or part; *public use* is limited to establishing public ownership only when it is absolutely necessary to provide essential state services; and *just compensation* requires paying market price for the property that is taken, and otherwise indemnifying the owner for any other loss he sustains as a result of the taking.

Government invokes economic *regulation* to obtain certain controls over private assets or enterprise. To a limited degree, regulation that restricts private economic activity is justified under a market economy. Few will reject regulation that actually secures public health and safety, prohibits noxious uses, and maintains law and order in real emergencies. It is important that government controls should be limited to forbidding private activity that truly violates the rights of others. The proper role of government is to protect the public from such harms, and not to prohibit or diminish individual production, competition or creativity.[105]

Chapter 5 sets forth a formula courts can apply for determining when regulation is constitutionally valid. However, regulation may become a taking of property, as explained in the prior section of this chapter under the heading "United States Experience." The general rule is that taking is effected when regulations become arbitrary or excessive.

The power of *taxation* must be applied equally and in ways that are not intended to confiscate property or enterprise, inhibit investment, or impose controls over property or business that would otherwise be prohibited. The prospect of high profits "drives the engine of economic development" and consequently high taxes create disincentives that seriously undermine development.[106] Taxation that cannot be justified as payment for benefits received constitutes in effect the taking of property.

Accordingly, to protect freedom and maximize investment opportunities, government must be severely limited in its powers of condemnation, regulation, and taxation.

## Protection of Property and Economic Liberties

One lesson to be drawn from the United States constitutional experience is the great need for careful drafting in the area of economic liberties. Although the Framers of the original Constitution and the Fourteenth Amendment sought to protect private ownership, investment, and enterprise, the United States Supreme Court has often in recent years not implemented those objectives—in part because the constitutional language is deficient or not clear in this respect.[107] For constitutional draftsmen seeking to secure property and economic rights, I suggest consideration of the following provisions.

> Private property and economic interests shall be secure from acquisition, control, possession, damage, or diminution by any branch, commission, agency, official, or officer of government, as follows:
>
> (1) (Property rights) Every person has the right, individually or in combination with others, to purchase, acquire, rent, own, use, mortgage, sell, lease, transfer, bequeath, and inherit private property, or any part or portion thereof. Private property includes any asset or thing of value, whether tangible or intangible, real or personal.
>
> (2) (Economic rights) Every person has the right, individually or in combination with others, freely to practice the occupation, profession, or trade of his or her choice, freely to establish, maintain, and operate a commercial enterprise, and freely to produce and distribute goods and services.
>
> (3) (Contract rights) Every person has the right, individually or in combination with others, to enter into binding agreements containing any and only provisions of their choice.

A constitution protecting property and economic interests should limit government ownership. Excepting that which it presently owns or operates, government should not own or operate any commercial enterprise. Government does not have the incentives or the skills required to obtain maximum benefits for the public from its ownership and investment. Not only is government not competent in this area, but it also has the incentive to pass laws that will restrict its private competitors, to the disadvantage of the public.

The emerging nations are seeking to privatize government owned enterprises, a most desirable objective and one that will be aided by constitutional provisions and laws that secure private owners against confiscation and oppressive regulation.

The national or any local government should not own any land or buildings except those to be used solely for absolutely essential public services, such as streets, public schools, and police and fire stations. In the event government seeks to purchase land or buildings for these purposes and the owner refuses to sell, a court should have power to enter an order conveying the property to the government but only upon its paying the owner full market value for the asset and full compensation for any economic loss sustained by the owner as a consequence of the government's action.

In 1856, a New York high court judge explained the legal meaning of ownership in a case that was of great importance in that period. While some regulation is possible, wrote Justice Comstock,

> where [property] rights are acquired by the citizen under the existing law, there is no power in any branch of the government to take them away; but where they are held contrary to the existing law, or are forfeited by its violation, then they may be taken from him—not by an act of the legislature, but in the due administration of the law itself, before the judicial tribunals of the state. The cause or occasion for depriving the citizen of his supposed rights must be found in the law as it is, or, at least it cannot be created by a legislative act which aims at their destruction. Where rights of property are admitted to exist, the legislature cannot say they shall exist no longer; nor will it make any difference, although a process and a tribunal are appointed to execute the sentence. If this is the "law of the land," and "due process of law," within the meaning of the constitution, then the legislature is omnipotent. It may, under the same interpretation, pass a law to take away liberty or life without a preexisting cause, appointing judicial and executive agencies to execute its will.[108]

The property right merits such strong protection because of its relation to freedom as well as to abundance, as previously discussed. A free society cannot exist unless government is prohibited from confiscating private property. If government can seize something owned by a private citizen, it can exert enormous power over people. One would be reluctant to speak, write, pray or petition in a manner displeasing to the authorities lest he lose what he has already earned and possesses.

As Hamilton stated, a power over a man's subsistence amounts to a power over his will.[109] U.S. Supreme Court Justice Joseph Story explained that the Constitution's just compensation requirement "is laid down by jurists as a principle of universal law [because] in a free government, almost all other rights would become utterly worthless, if the government possessed an uncontrollable power over the private fortune of every citizen."[110]

## II Regulating Economic Activity

### *United States Experience*

For a lengthy period in United States history, the Supreme Court safeguarded economic activity from restraint by the state and federal governments. Between 1897 and 1937 under the doctrine of substantive or economic due process, the court invalidated many laws that needlessly or unnecessarily limited freedom of enterprise.

Among the noteworthy laws that the court struck down then as violating either the due process or equal protection clauses of the United States Constitution were a New York statute limiting the working hours of bakery employees to 60 per week or 10 per day, an Oklahoma law enabling a state commission to limit entry into the ice making business, a New York act imposing price controls on theater ticket resales, a Nebraska statute prohibiting employment agencies from collecting fees from employees, and a Pennsylvania law that effectively banned chain drugstores from the state. Today all of these laws probably would be upheld by the Supreme Court.

The period of spectacular economic growth in the United States around the turn of this century was also the time when judicial protection of economic liberties was most vigilant. Every individual and corporate entrepreneur could then claim the protection of the federal constitution against federal, state and local restrictions that limited economic activity and opportunity. And the burden was on the government to prove that its attempted regulation did not arbitrarily limit economic activity.

The economic due process era lasted about 40 years. During that period, the U.S. wealth grew at an awesome rate; by 1914, the national income exceeded that of the United Kingdom, Germany, France, Austria-Hungary, and Italy combined and the per capita income was by far the highest in the world.[111] Moreover, real wages were rising and working hours declining.

Wholesale and consumer prices were virtually the same in 1914–15 as in 1840, while wage rates per hour for all industries other than agriculture for which data are available rose three-fold for this period.[112] The average work hours per week in all manufacturing industries declined from 60 in 1890 to 50.3 in 1926.[113] It has been estimated that an increase of 63 percent in the per capita real income of the working population occurred between 1850 and 1900 and that an 18 percent increase occurred between 1900 and 1929.[114]

Because few welfare laws and unions existed during these decades, this betterment of life must be attributed to the success of the economic system.

Although poverty and material inequalities continued, the system appeared to function remarkably well. It was thus not difficult to conclude that this success could be undermined by restricting entrepreneurial freedom—that which harms business also injures the livelihoods of workers and consumers. The Supreme Court's concept of liberty enabled the process to continue providing a great measure of economic benefits.

In those years, the opposition to economic due process came largely from critics demanding social reforms and income redistributions, which could be achieved only by Congress and the state legislatures. They viewed the judiciary as a serious impediment to such ends. What the reformers apparently did not comprehend was that while judicial review would annul some welfare measures, it would also dispose of legislation favorable to the rich and special interest groups. Although legislatures pass statutes intended to help the disadvantaged, they also impose regulations that serve the wealthy and small special interest groups at the expense of the poor. (See pages 45–50, *supra.*)

However, for the liberal-oriented justices on the Supreme Court in the 1930s, economic salvation existed in the political process, and abruptly, the constitutional protection of economic liberty was withdrawn. The dissatisfaction with the economic system caused by the worldwide depression of the 1930s spawned regulatory schemes of all kinds; and the court after a brief defense, capitulated. The majority of justices declared themselves willing to approve any legislative regulatory program so long as it was not arbitrary or capricious and did not infringe on some other constitutionally protected rights (such as freedom of the press). Beginning in late 1930s, the court adopted an even more deferential policy. In economic matters, the court said the legislature had merely to seem to act in a rational manner; the burden of proof was on the complainant to show that it had not. Reversal of the earlier priorities was complete: economic regulation was now clearly acceptable, and freedom from it the exception.

Yet, for many in society, the opportunity to engage freely in a business, trade, occupation, or profession is the most important liberty society has to offer. Moreover, it is a liberty that provides immense benefits to the society.

Nevertheless, regardless of its merits, economic due process is not likely to return to this country at the federal level for the foreseeable future. A major reason for this is that many in the legal community believe that the United States Constitution does not authorize it. They assert that the framers of the due process and equal protection clauses never intended to empower the judiciary to protect economic liberties pursuant to these provisions. Included in this group are strong advocates of private enterprise;

often the issue does not divide scholars on the basis of liberal and conservative perspectives.[115] In my opinion, the Constitution does provide such protection, and I have presented this position in my book, *Economic Liberties and the Constitution.*[116]

## Limiting the Legislature

Let us consider how in the economic area a constitutional court should decide when regulations shall be sustained or annulled. As previously explained, courts in the United States and western countries have developed rules for this purpose. In chapter 5, I have listed these rules for insertion in a constitution. As an example of how some of these rules operate with respect to restraints on economic activities, reflect on the situation presented in the case of *Minnesota v. Clover Leaf Creamery Co.*[117] This case involved a 1977 Minnesota law prohibiting the retail sale of milk in plastic, non-returnable, non-refillable containers. The sale of milk in paperboard cartons was not affected. The plastic bottle manufacturers and retailers sued to declare the law unconstitutional on the basis that it denied them their liberties to produce and distribute plastic milk bottles, a legitimate item of commerce.

The first issue considered by the trial court was whether the law serves important government objectives.[118] To recapitulate, economic regulations are imposed for one or both of the following reasons: first, to cause the economic system to function better—that is, to remedy or remove the excesses or limitations of the private market; second, to secure an economic advantage for a person, corporation or group by the elimination or obstruction of competing businesses, occupations, products or services.

If the court finds the second reason is controlling in a particular situation, then the law in question does not serve important governmental objectives. Not only does it deny liberty, it also reduces production and competition and thereby increases costs, disadvantaging the vast majority and benefiting only a small number. It takes from A and gives to B for the benefit of B. In the Minnesota bottle case, the state trial court found that the "actual basis for the act" was to promote the interests of (1) certain parts of the local dairy industry and (2) the pulpwood industry and harm the interests of (1) other segments of the dairy industry and (2) the plastics industry. It accordingly held the law unconstitutional.

However, suppose the court finds that the law seeks to increase competition and productivity, to eliminate waste or to improve the environment. These are important governmental objectives and meet the first test. The next issue is whether the law will substantially achieve these objectives—the means-ends test. The Minnesota Supreme Court, unlike the trial court, assumed that the purpose of the bottle law was legitimate—to enhance the environment, to conserve energy and resources, and so on—but would not achieve these purposes. Therefore, the restraint on liberty was without purpose, and futile. The law failed to pass the second requirement of the formula—the fit between means and ends must be close—and consequently was unconstitutional on this basis.

As discussed in Chapter 5, there also may be alternative, less restrictive laws that the legislature might pass to achieve the same purposes, or the consequences of the law might be too severe to warrant the benefits. In either event, liberty is being unduly restricted and the law should be annulled. None of the courts adjudicating the Minnesota controversy passed on these issues.

## III Provisions on Taxation and Spending

Like regulation, taxation can also strangle the economy. The amount of the tax burden is one factor an investor will consider in deciding whether or not to invest. Taxes add to the cost of production and cost of living. The greater the total taxes, the greater the negative impact on work, investment and ownership. For example, if taxes lower the investor's net return by 50%, the deterrent impact will be much greater than at 20%.

If investment is reduced as a result of taxation or goes into the tax-free underground economy, the country's tax revenues may be lowered. Consider the experience of this nation. The income tax rate reductions in the United States in the 1980s and 1960s increased the income tax revenues collected from the rich and lowered the amount of taxes paid by others. In the 1980s, Congress decreased rates and made other changes in the tax laws reducing considerably individual tax liability. The tax revenues collected from the top 10 percent of earners rose from $150.6 billion in 1981 to $199.8 billion in 1988, an increase of 32.7 percent measured in constant dollars. For the top five percent of earners, the increase in tax revenues collected for this period was 44.1 percent. Total tax revenues for this period increased by 11.7 percent in constant dollars.[119] The percent of all taxes that the top ten percent paid rose from 49.3 percent in 1980 to 57.2 percent in 1988.[120]

Similarly, after the 1964 tax cut of about 20 percent, the revenues collected from the top five percent of earners rose from $17.17 billion in 1963 to $18.49 billion in 1965, an increase of 7.7 percent in constant dollars. Total tax revenues for this period slightly decreased by 0.3 percent.[121]

The increased tax collections from the rich as herein reported are largely attributable to greater risk taking by them which was encouraged by the tax reductions. The avoidance by the rich of tax shelters and lavish tax deductible expenses may have also increased their tax payments.

According to Polyconomics, an economics consulting firm, between 1984 and 1989, of 23 countries with developed economies, the highest growth rates were recorded by those with the lowest "marginal tax rates," defined as a weighted combination of the top marginal tax rates on labor and capital. At the extremes were Denmark with an 80.2 "marginal tax rate" and a gross national product real growth rate of 8 percent and Hong Kong with comparative rates of 15.9 and 97 percent.[122]

Taxes have an adverse impact on the incentive to invest and work, economic efficiency and aggregate output. Thus, New York economists Stephen Kagann and Zheng Gu found that during a recessionary period, if the tax burden is already high, each $100 million in new taxes in New York City will lead to the loss of approximately 11,400 private-sector jobs citywide.[123]

Recognizing the impediments of taxation, a great many countries in recent years reduced considerably their maximum marginal tax rates on personal income. High tax rates remain an international problem. Mexico, for example, reduced its top income tax rate from 60 to 35 percent; yet it has been estimated that collected revenues in that country are only 15 percent of what they would be if the government enacted lower rates and simplified the tax code.[124]

Spending to achieve the collective good is counterproductive when it requires taxation that limits significantly economic output—and thereby of course the collective good. Because the pressures for government spending are very great in democratic countries, constitutional controls over spending and taxes are essential. John Randolph, an early American political leader, referred to "the most delicious of privileges" as that of spending other people's money. Some politicians facetiously assert that only women should be legislators because nature has endowed them with the will to say no. More seriously, constitutional restraints on spending are required to control politicians' natural tendencies to please the voters.

Some emerging states recognize the adverse impact of taxation. Thus under Article 32 of Ukraine's law on foreign investment, enterprises with foreign investment and participation of Ukrainian capital are exempt from income taxation for from two to five years after the declaration of the first income, and thereafter are required to pay taxes at the rate of 50 to 70 percent of the required tax rates. Ukraine provides various other tax reductions and exemptions encouraging investment by foreign and domestic interests.[125]

Constitutions should not prescribe tax systems or programs. This is the responsibility of the elected branches of government. But a constitution must protect the people from confiscatory and arbitrary laws, regardless of the subject of these laws. In the United States, serious efforts have for many years been undertaken to curb taxes at the state level. Probably the strongest effort was by Oklahoma voters in 1992 requiring that a tax measure must be adopted by vote of three-quarters of each house of the legislature. Otherwise, it must be submitted for public approval by the voters.

Accordingly, the following are suggested constitutional provisions limiting taxation and spending:

1. The maximum amount of annual taxes on real property or on a commercial venture shall not exceed ____ percent of the full market value of such property or venture. California's constitution limits the maximum amount of ad valorem taxes on real property to one percent of its full cash value.[126]

2. The total amount of taxes collected in any one year shall not exceed a specific percentage of the gross national income of the nation for the prior year, except with the consent of two-thirds of the legislature.

3. The national government shall not incur indebtedness or liability in any manner or for any purpose exceeding in any year the income and revenues received for such year, except with the consent of two-thirds of the legislature.

4. When for any year, total revenues received by the government exceeds total outlays, the surplus shall be used to reduce the amount levied for subsequent years.

5. The president or chief executive officer of the nation should have the power to veto specific taxes or spending items either as part of a general or a specific veto power. This power is referred to as a line item veto. The legislature should be able to override such a veto with a two-thirds majority.

A major failing of the Communist systems was their spending practices which displayed little consideration for the yield from and cost to existing resources. A different perspective must prevail under a market system. At reasonably full employment, natural and human resources used for government directed purposes cannot be devoted to private activities, limiting the scope of the private market upon which a nation is primarily dependent for progress and abundance.

# 7
# Protecting Solely Liberties and Not Entitlements

The United States Constitution has often been referred to as a bill of rights, and there are two reasons in theory for this: First, the government has no authority to deprive persons of their liberties. Second, persons are guaranteed liberties to engage in activities of their choice.

These protections are negative in character; they are intended to negate laws that restrict the exercise of human liberties. The United States Constitution does not impose affirmative economic obligations on either the government or the private sector. Unlike some constitutions, it does not provide entitlements for housing, education and medical service, and does not mandate owners and entrepreneurs to maintain certain employment conditions, such as minimum wages and hours. Under the United States Constitution, providing for the collective good is the responsibility of the legislature (not the courts), which it must exercise with due regard for individual liberties. Judge Richard Posner asserts the following:

> The men who wrote the Bill of Rights were not concerned that government might do too little for the people but that it might do too much to them. The Fourteenth Amendment, adopted in 1868 at the height of laissez-faire thinking, sought to protect Americans from oppression by state government, not to secure them basic governmental services.[127]

Liberty in the United States Constitutional sense, means being immune from government coercion. However, to provide for entitlements and private economic standards requires subordinating individual freedom to the collective good. Liberties and entitlements may at times be in direct conflict, for bestowing an entitlement may require eliminating or diminishing a liberty. Thus, to implement entitlements for some, government may take property or other resources from one group and transfer it to another, an action which may violate liberties.

A constitution that protects both liberties and entitlements is incoherent and very difficult to interpret. It seeks to accomplish two diametrically opposite goals. Moreover, guarantees of entitlements in a constitution that provides for judicial review will jeopardize the judiciary's protection of liberty. To enforce entitlements, the judiciary might mandate imposition of taxation and spending, and neither the people nor the legislature would be able to control this power. The judiciary would be given control over important fiscal decisions.[128] Taxing the people and spending the receipts are peculiarly legislative powers, stemming from the idea that only the people, acting on their own or through their representatives, are entitled to decide how they will utilize their own funds.

> Surely this decision, about the adequacy of welfare payments, is one that will change through time and must be adjusted according to the willingness of the population to bear the tax burdens involved. It is not the sort of thing that can be fixed by judges according to the invariant standard of justice that we rely upon the courts to apply. It is not a matter for judicial determination; it is a matter for parliamentary debate.[129]

Similarly, a court may implement provisions in a constitution that require a clean environment and adequate standards of living by imposing personal monetary requirements that reduce and limit the property or contract rights of owners and entrepreneurs.

A constitution that guaranties both liberties and entitlements does not send an attractive message to investors. Given constitutional commitments to welfare, social and environmental benefits, potential investors may question the reliability of the nation's commitments against confiscation, and excessive regulation and taxation. In the world wide competition to attract business and industry, countries that give constitutional priority to entitlements are likely to suffer disadvantage over those who do not.

It is not wise to accord the judiciary what is basically a legislative power to provide monetary and social benefits for the public. Judges do not have the same options as legislators, who can choose among a great number of competing interests and values. Courts decide only the matters that are submitted to them for adjudication. They do not have the option of determining, for example, how much taxes should be collected and how much should be spent; they cannot determine the amount of funds that should be designated for welfare or any other purpose, and how the welfare or other budgets should be allocated among competing interests. In the words of the United States Supreme Court:

[T]he intractable economic, social and even philosophical problems presented by public welfare assistance programs are not the business of this Court. . . . [T]he Constitution does not empower this Court to second-guess state officials charged with the difficult responsibility of allocating limited public welfare funds among the myriad of potential recipients.[130]

For the same reasons, judges should not decide how owners or entrepreneurs operate their businesses or allocate their resources. Nor can it be maintained that courts are better situated to solve societal problems than politically dominated legislatures, since solutions in these areas usually involve ideology and personal predilection.

In the words of Alexander Hamilton, the judiciary under the United States Constitution, has no influence over either the sword or the purse,

no direction either of the strength or wealth of the society, and [could] take no active resolution whatever. It may truly be said to have neither FORCE nor WILL but merely judgment; and must ultimately depend on the aid of the executive arm even for the efficacy of its judgments.[131]

The province of the judiciary is not to undertake wealth redistributions; its role is limited to insuring that when the legislature engages in such tasks, it does not do so at the expense of individual liberties. The court has a role in progress, equality and redistribution. But it is one that is tied to individual achievement, initiative, and creativity. As a protector of individual liberties, the court assures society that private people, as the major source of progress will continue, individually or in concert, to be free to apply themselves to undertakings of their own choice.

The recently adopted Czech and Slovak charter previously referred to protects both liberties and entitlements. However, the document does not provide for judicial enforcement of the entitlements. Article 41(1) provides: "The rights listed [in articles granting entitlements] may be claimed only within the scope of the laws implementing these provisions." This approach is much more satisfactory than one which permits judicial enforcement, and may be necessary to accommodate political pressures for constitutional recognition of entitlements. As has been observed, for all practical purposes Article 41(1) downgrades entitlements "from rights to aspirations and exhortations to the legislature."[132]

Nevertheless, there is a problem in constitutionally identifying entitlements as rights. Even when the judiciary is denied enforcement powers, the judges may give special weight to such constitutional assertions in evaluating personal protections. Moreover, a legally unsophisticated public may criticize a judiciary which protects only certain constitutional rights and not all of them. Regrettably, respect for the process of judicial review might seriously suffer as a result.

Entitlements and other public benefits are matters of concern for the legislature. A constitution might set forth these legislative aspirations along these lines:

> Within the limitations imposed by this constitution, the National Assembly shall in its best discretion and highest wisdom seek to improve and elevate the people's health, safety, well being and living conditions, advance and encourage education and culture, tax and spend for the common good and public interest, protect and preserve personal security and family life, enhance the environment, and safeguard the people from their domestic and foreign enemies.

# 8
# Amending the Constitution

It is very difficult to amend the United States Constitution. Article V sets forth two procedures for obtaining amendments. First, the proposed amendment must be passed initially by two-thirds vote of each house of Congress. Then it must be submitted to the states, and is considered ratified when the legislatures or special constitutional conventions in three-quarters of the states approve. Second, two-thirds of the states must request Congress to call a constitutional convention to consider a proposed amendment. Any amendment recommended by the convention must be approved by three-quarters of the states.

As a constitutional advisor to that nation, I recommended that the new Bulgarian constitution be made difficult to amend on the theory that people should be able to act in reliance on it. The Bulgarian constitution established in 1991 is difficult to amend—it requires a three-quarters vote of the legislature, and this can only be achieved if both major parties approve the amendment.

Critics fear many provisions of the Bulgarian constitution will ill-serve the country. Even assuming this to be the case, I am still inclined to agree with the idea that amendments should not come about easily. A constitution that can be readily changed is more of a law than a constitution. By its very meaning, a constitution must be enduring. As the interpreter of the document, the judiciary should be able to smooth some of the rough ridges without changing essential meaning. One lesson of the Bulgarian constitutional experience is that the final draft of the document should be submitted for widespread consideration and discussion before it is approved, something which apparently did not occur in that country.

Requiring public approval of the constitution would open it to additional discussion and consideration. During the ratification period of the United States Constitution, the public demanded as a condition for ratification that the Constitution's supporters promise to amend the constitution once it was approved to include a Bill of Rights. Thus, ratification debates may bring to light major constitutional deficiencies.

Another suggestion for reducing textual errors or construction problems is that provision be made for a general constitutional review five to ten years after ratification. The difficulty with this proposal is that investors might be influenced to make their decisions with this time schedule in mind. However, the idea offers reasonable compromise for the various concerns at issue.

# 9
# Concluding Observations

In recent years, our world has experienced an extraordinary historical event that few if any had ever forecast: almost simultaneously, millions of people in many countries shed despotism in favor of freedom. They demolished a system which smothered their humanity and foreclosed their opportunity for progress and betterment. In the entire history of freedom, there has never has been so great an advance within so brief a period.

What a horrible tragedy it would be if governments were now established that would return these people to the oppressions from which they escaped. I do not speak idly for I have observed and listened to American advisors who counsel the adoption of constitutions and laws that might bring about such a terrible result.

It should by now be clear that these revolutions were against an evil system and not evil rulers. They were intended to minimize the rule of the state and maximize the freedom of the people. Those who now advocate establishing a huge governmental role in the economies of these nations do not comprehend the meaning of what has occurred.

Government should be powerful enough to protect the people against their foreign and local enemies and domestic perils and excesses. It must never be powerful enough to oppress the people or inhibit their wisdom and productivity. In the words of the United States Supreme Court,

> To sustain the individual freedom of action contemplated by the [United States] Constitution, is not to strike down the common good but to exalt it; for surely the good of society as a whole cannot be better served than by the preservation against arbitrary restraint of the liberties of its constituent members.[133]

The great lesson of modern times is the strong relationship between freedom and progress. Maximizing freedom will also maximize a nation's philosophical, cultural and material resources.

Principles of freedom should guide the liberated nations and republics in framing their constitutions. A constitution is the most important legal document for a nation that subscribes to the rule of law. In its constitution, a nation defines the relationship between the people and their government. In rejecting tyranny, the people of Eastern and Central Europe have salvaged and preserved the rights to which they are entitled as human beings. They should now constitutionally enshrine these rights forever.

# Notes

[1] *See* Zbigniew Brezezinski, "The Grand Failure: The Birth and Death of Communism in the Twentieth Century" (New York: Charles Scribner's Sons, 1989).

[2] The author was a member of Bulgarian Economic Growth and Transition Project, commissioned by the National Chamber Foundation in 1990, and authored the Project's recommendations for a new constitution.

[3] Constitution of the Republic of Bulgaria, established by the Grand National Assembly on July 12, 1991.

[4] 3 Max Farrand, "The Records of the Federal Convention of 1787" at 85 (rev.ed. 1937) (New Haven Conn., and London: Yale Univ. Press 1966).

[5] Brezezinski, *supra* note 1, at 165–166.

[6] "The Federalist Papers" No. 84 at 513–514 (A. Hamilton) (A Mentor Book, 1961).

[7] John Locke, "Two Treatises of Government," Second Treatise, ch. XI, sec. 137 (Chicago: Henry Regnery, 1955).

[8] *Id.* sec. 138. Locke defined property as including "Lives, Liberties and Estates." *Id.* sec. 123. It was not confined to material possessions.

[9] 1 W. Blackstone, "Commentaries on the Laws of England," 125, 130, 134, 140 (1765).

[10] This view is consistent with the "public choice" perspective advanced by James M. Buchanan, Nobel Laureate in Economics for 1986. He emphasizes self interest as the motivating factor in both private and political choice. However, the forces of the economics marketplace are more likely to channel individual self interest into socially desirable outcomes. *See generally* James Buchanan & Gordon Tullock, "The Calculus of Consent: Logical Foundations of Constitutional Democracy" (1965).

[11] "The Federalist Papers" No. 51 at 322 (J. Madison) (A Mentor Book, 1961).

[12] *See generally,* Bernard Siegan, *Separation of Powers and Other Divisions of Authority Under the Constitution,* 23 Suffolk U. L. Rev. 1 (1989).

[13] "The Federalist Papers" No. 47 at 301 (J. Madison) (A. Mentor Book, 1961).

[14] INS v. Chada, 462 U.S. 919, 959 (1983).

[15]*See generally* Gerald W. Scully, *The Institutional Framework and Economic Development*, 96 Journ. Pol. Econ. 952 (1988).

[16]"The Federalist Papers" No. 73 at 443 (A. Hamilton) (A. Mentor Book, 1961). *See* discussion of the President's Power of Veto, Chapter 2.

[17]"The Federalist Papers" No. 78 at 466 (A. Hamilton) (A Mentor Book, 1961).

[18]Charles Grove Haines, "The American Doctrine of Judicial Supremacy" 209–10 (2d ed., Russell & Russell 1959).

[19]"The Federalist Papers" No. 48, at 309 (J. Madison) (A Mentor Book, 1961). Madison quoted Jefferson as criticizing the Virginia legislature as "in *many* instances, *decid[ing] rights* which should have been left to *judiciary controversy.*" Id. at 311.

[20]25 "The Papers Of Alexander Hamilton," 479 (H. Syrett ed. 1977).

[21]1 M. Farrand, *supra* note 4, at 512.

[22]*Id.* at 51.

[23]United States v. Lovett, 328 U.S. 303 (1946); Brown v. United States, 381 U.S. 437 (1965).

[24]1 W. Blackstone, *supra* note 9 at 46.

[25]Dash v. Van Kleeck, 7 Johns. (N.Y.) 477, 506 (1811).

[26]"Government hardly could go on if to some extent values incident to property could not be diminished without paying for every such change in the general law." Justice Oliver Wendell Holmes, Jr. in Pennsylvania Coal Co. v. Mahon, 260 U.S. 393, 413 (1922).

[27]United Jewish Organizations of Williamsburgh v. Carey, 430 U.S. 144 (1977).

[28]The French Constitution, adopted Sept. 28, 1958, as amended, Title II.

[29]John Locke, "Two Treatises of Government," Second Treatise, ch. XI, Sec. 142 (Chicago: Henry Regnery, 1955).

[30]United States v. Robel, 389 U.S. 258, 276 (1967) (concurring opinion).

[31]*See* Panama Refining Co. v. Ryan, 293 U.S. 388 (1935); Schechter Poultry Corp. v. United States, 295 U.S. 495 (1935); Field v. Clark, 143 U.S. 649 (1892); United States v. Grimaud, 220 U.S. 506, 517 (1911).

[32]Field v. Clark, 143 U.S. 649 (1892).

[33]The French Constitution, adopted Sept. 28, 1958, Art. 56.

[34]Jon Elster, *Constitutionalism in Eastern Europe: An Introduction*, 58 Univ. of Chicago L.Rev. 447, 465 (1991); Lloyd Cutler and Herman Schwartz, *Constitutional Reform in Czechoslovakia*, 58 Univ. Chicago L.Rev. 511, 538–44 (1991).

[35]*See* Taylor v. Porter, 4 Hill 140, 145–46 (N.Y. 1843).

[36]*See* Kenneth J. Arrow, "Social Choice and Individual Values" (New York: John Wiley and Sons, 1966); Duncan Black, "The Theory of Committees and Elections" (Cambridge, Ma.: Cambridge University Press, 1958); William Riker and Peter J. Ordeshook, "An Introduction to Positive-Political Theory" (Englewood Cliffs, N.J.: Prentice-Hall, 1973).

[37]1 Alexis de Tocqueville, "Democracy in America" 249 (New Rochelle, N.Y.: Arlington House 1965).

[38]"The Federalist Papers" No. 51 at 324 (A. Hamilton) (A Mentor Book, 1961).

[39]Milton & Rose Friedman, "Free to Choose" 129-30 (New York & London: Harcourt Brace Jovanovich, 1979).

[40]*See* Bernard H. Siegan, *Commentary on Monahan Paper,* 21 Univ. British Columbia L. Rev. 165 (1987).

[41]Texas v. Johnson, 109 S.Ct. 2533 (1989).

[42]Griswold v. Connecticut, 381 U.S. 479 (1985).

[43]DeShaney v. Winnebago County Dept. of Social Servs., 109 S.Ct. 998, 1003 (1989).

[44]394 U.S. 618 (1969).

[45]411 U.S. 1 (1973).

[46]432 U.S. 464 (1977).

[47]488 U.S. 297 (1980).

[48]457 U.S. 202 (1982).

[49]108 S.Ct. 248 (1988).

[50]Meriwether v. Garrett, 102 U.S. 472, 521 (1880) (Field, J., concurring).

[51]Bernard H. Siegan, *Majorities May Limit the People's Liberties Only When Authorized to Do So by the Constitution,* 27 Univ. San Diego L.Rev. 309, 310-319 (1990).

[52]U.S. Const. Amend. IX.

[53]1 W. Blackstone, *supra* note 9, at 121-122 (1765).

[54]McCulloch v. Maryland, 17 U.S. (4 Wheat.) 316, 421 (1819).

[55]*See,* for example, David C. McDonald, "Legal Rights in the Canadian Charter of Rights and Freedoms" (Toronto, Calgary & Vancouver: The Carswell Company Limited, 2nd Ed. 1989).

[56]Constitution of the People's Republic of Bulgaria, adopted by national referendum on May 16, 1971. Article 1(2) grants special status to the nation's communist party: "The guiding force in society and the state is the Bulgarian Communist Party."

[57]Slaughter-House Cases, 83 U.S. (16 Wall.) 36, 115 (1873) (Bradley, J., dissenting).

[58]Cutler and Schwartz, *supra,* note 34 at 536, referring to art. 4(4).

[59]Pennsylvania Coal Co. v. Mahon, 260 U.S. 393, 415 (1922).

[60]Employment Division v. Smith, 494 U.S. 872 (1990) O'Connor, J., dissenting).

[61]Law of Ukraine on Foreign Investments (Apr. 1992).

[62]H. Wechsler, *Toward Neutral Principles of Constitutional Law,* 73 Harv. L.Rev. 1, 19 (1959).

[63] The dilemma of resolving the tension between the majority and a minority has been referred to as the *Madisonian Dilemma* because it is inherent in the United States Constitution of which Madison was the leading author. It is the subject of many theories of constitutional law. *See* Robert H. Bork, "The Tempting of America," 139-141 (New York and London: The Free Press, 1990).

[64]U.S. Const. Amendment XIV, Sec. 1.

[65]83 U.S. (16 Wall.) 36 (1873).

[66]H. J. Graham, "Everyman's Constitution" 319 (New York: Norton, 1968).

[67]*See* Chapter 4, III "Protection of Liberty."

[68]*See* text accompanying note 53.

[69]Craig v. Boren, 429 U.S. 190, 221 (1976) (Rehnquist, J., dissenting).

[70]The Supreme Court of Canada holds that the objective must be "of sufficient importance to warrant overriding a constitutionally protected right or freedom. The standard must be high in order to ensure that objectives which are trivial or discordant with the principles integral to a free and democratic society do not gain [constitutional] protection. It is necessary, at a minimum, that an objective relate to concerns which are pressing and substantial in a free and democratic society before it can be characterized as sufficiently important." R. v. Oakes, 1 S.C.R. 103, 138–39 (1986).

However, Roger Pilon asserts that the government's power to limit rights without compensation should be confined to stopping injury to personal or property rights. "[W]hen the activity prohibited is a rights violating activity, no compensation is required, for the activity is illegitimate to begin with ... [W]hen the activity is legitimate, the state has no right to prohibit it." Activity injuring life, liberty, or property, broadly construed, would constitute illegitimate activity. Roger Pilon, *Property Rights and a Free Society,* in "Resolving the Housing Crisis," 369, 379–391 (Cambridge, Ma: Balinger Publ. Co., 1982, M. Bruce Johnson, ed.).

[71]*See* R. v. Morgentaler, 1 S.C.R. 30, 73–74 (1988); R. v. Oakes, 1 S.C.R. 103, 139 (1986).

[72]Nebbia v. New York, 291 U.S. 502, 556 (1933) (McReynolds, J., dissenting).

[73]Schenck v. United States, 249 U.S. 47, 52 (1919).

[74]*See* McDonald, *supra* note 55 at 71–104. Article 29(2) of the UN General Assembly's Universal Declaration of Human Rights provides a standard by which to decide the validity of restraints on human rights. For the reasons set forth in this chapter, I believe the four-pronged analysis preferable to the Declaration's provision that limitations may be imposed

> solely for the purpose of securing due recognition and respect for the rights and freedoms of others and of meeting the just requirements of morality, public order and the general welfare in a democratic society.

[75]R. v. Oakes, 1 S.C.R. 103 (1986).

[76]*See* Bernard H. Siegan, "Economic Liberties and the Constitution," 324–26 (Chicago: Univ. of Chicago Press, 1980).

[77]Nebbia v. New York, 291 U.S. 502, 548 (1934) (Mc Reynolds, J., dissenting).

[78]Gerald Gunther, *The Supreme Court 1971 Term, Forward: In Search of Evolving Doctrine on a Changing Court: A Model for a Newer Equal Protection,* 86 Harv. L.Rev. 1, 8 (1972).

[79]*See* Bernard H. Siegan, "The Supreme Court's Constitution: An Inquiry Into Judicial Review and Its Impact on Society" 154–155 (New Brunswick, N.J.: Transaction Books, 1987).

[80]Scully, *supra* note 15.

[81]J. Gwartney, W. Block, and R. Lawson, *Measuring Economic Freedom,* in "Rating Global Economic Freedom" 153–229 (Vancouver, B.C.: Fraser Institute, 1992. S. T. Easton and M. Walker, eds.).

[82]*Id.*

[83]T. Kamm, *Chile's Economy Roars as Exports Take Off in Post-Pinochet Era,* Wall St. Journ. Jan. 25, 1993, p.1, col. 1; C. Singer, *Why Chile's Economy Roared While the World's Slumbered,* Wall St. Journ. Jan. 22, 1993, p. A15, col. 3.

[84]Siegan, *supra* note 76, 283-303.

[85]Ronald Coase, *Economists and Public Policy,* in "Large Corporations in a Changing Society," 184 (New York: New York University Press, 1974. J. Fred Weston, Ed.).

[86]*Id.*

[87]James D. Gwartney and Richard L. Stroup, "Economics Public and Private Choice," 94, 743, 753-55 (Harcourt Brace Jovanovich, 5th ed., 1989).

[88]Richard Posner, "Economic Analysis of Law," 405 (Boston and Toronto: Little, Brown, 2d Ed. 1977).

[89]Michael Granfield, *Changing Industries and Economic Performance* in "Large Corporations in a Changing Society," *supra* note 85, at 164.

[90]Thomas A. Hopkins, *Cost of Regulation,* A Rochester Institute of Technology Working Paper (Rochester, N.Y., Dec. 1991). *See* Robert W. Hahn and John A. Hird, *The Costs and Benefits of Regulation: Review and Synthesis,* 8 Yale Journ. on Regulation 233 (1991); Robert E. Litan and William D. Nordhaus, "Reforming Federal Regulation" (New Haven: Yale Univ. Press, 1983); Murray L. Weidenbaum, *The Costs of Government Regulation of Business,* A Study for the Joint Economic Committee, Congress of the United States, April 10, 1978.

[91]482 U.S. 304 (1987).

[92]483 U.S. 825 (1987).

[93]112 S.Ct. 2886 (1992).

[94]483 U.S. at 836 n. 4.

[95]Loretto v. Teleprompter Manhattan CATV Corp., 458 U.S. 419 (1982).

[96]Second Restatement of Torts, § 821-§ 829.

[97]112 S.Ct. at 2903 (Kennedy, J., concurring).

[98]1 W. Blackstone *supra* note 9 at 139.

[99]United States v. General Motors Corp., 323 U.S. 373, 378 (1945).

[100]Pumpelly v. Green Bay Co., 80 U.S. 166, 177-178 (1872).

[101]Seawall Associates v. City of New York, 74 N.Y.2d 92 (1989).

[102]In effect, the owners were denied their investment-backed expectations to operate a particular use; however, the court did not rule on this issue.

[103]482 U.S. at 321, citing Pennsylvania Coal Co. v. Mahon, 260 U.S. at 416 (1922).

[104]U.S. Const. Amend. V: "nor shall private property be taken for public use without just compensation."

[105]*See* Bernard H. Siegan, Conserving and Developing the Land, 27 U.S.D. Law Rev. 279 (1990).

[106]*See* Charles E. McLure, Jr., "Income Tax Policy for the Russian Republic," 3 (Stanford, Ca.: Hoover Institution, Stanford University, 1991).

[107]*See generally,* Siegan *supra* note 76.

[108]Wynehamer v. People, 13 N.Y. 378, 393 (1956).

[109]"The Federalist Papers" No. 79 at 472 (A. Hamilton) (A Mentor Book, 1961).

[110]3 Joseph Story, "Commentaries on the Constitution" 661 (New York: Da Capo Press, 1970).

[111]Chester Whitney Wright, "Economic History of the United States," 429, 889 (New York: McGraw-Hill, 2d Ed. 1949).

[112]George F. Warren & Frank Pearson, "Gold and Prices," 316–317 (New York: John Wiley & Sons, 1935); Bureau of Labor Statistics, "History of Wages in the United States from Colonial Times to 1928" at 521 (Washingon, D.C.: Gov't Printing Office, 1934); "The Statistical History of the United States from Colonial Times to the Present" at 211 (New York: Basic Books, 1976).

[113]Paul H. Douglas, "Real Wages in the United States 1890–1926" at 116 (New York: Augustus M. Kelley, 1926).

[114]Wright, *supra* note 111 at 890.

[115]*See* Robert H. Bork, "The Tempting of America," (New York: The Free Press, 1990).

[116]*Supra*, note 76.

[117]449 U.S. 456 (1981). The United States Supreme Court sustained the Minnesota statute which was declared unconstitutional for the reasons explained in the text by both the trial and Supreme Court of the state.

[118]Clover Leaf Creamery Company v. State of Minnesota, District Ct., County of Ramsey, No. 423258 (Apr. 5, 1978). Unlike the test of "legitimate objective" recommended in chapter 5, the Minnesota trial court used the higher standard of "*important* government objective." cf. *supra* pg. 40.

[119]James D. Gwartney and Richard L. Stroup, "Economics Public and Private Choice," 117–120 (Harcourt Brace Jovanovich, 6th ed., 1992).

[120]Gwartney and Stroup, *The 1980s Tax Cuts: Welfare for the Rich?,* The Detroit News, May 11, 1992.

[121]Gwartney and Stroup, Fifth Edition (1981) *supra* note 119 at 118–119.

[122]Source: Polyconomics, Inc., Morristown, N.J., report dated Mar. 31, 1992.

[123]Stephen Kagann, *New York's Vanishing Supply Side,* The City Journ. (Autumn 1992).

[124]David Asman, *The Salinas Reforms Take Root,* Wall St. Journal, Dec. 2, 1991.

[125]Law of Ukraine on Foreign Investments (Apr. 1992).

[126]Constitution of California, Art. IIIA, Sec. 1 (1983).

[127]Jackson v. City of Joliet, 715 F.2d 1200, 1203 (7th Cir., 1983).

[128]A recent United States Supreme Court case illustrates the problem. Upon finding that the Kansas City, Missouri, School District operated a segregated school district in violation of the Constitution, the trial court issued a desegregation order containing details of the financing necessary to implement a remedy. As part of the remedy, the court ordered the school district's property tax levy to be raised from $2.05 to $4.20 per $100 of assessed valuation. The United States Supreme Court unanimously held that the trial judge had abused his discretion in imposing the tax. The 5–4 majority asserted, however, that a court order directing a local government body to levy its own taxes is constitutional. Missouri v. Jenkins, 495 U.S. 33 (1990).

The insertion of entitlement rights in a Constitution risks judicial intervention of this character.

[129]M. Walker, *Some Principles for Constitutional Change,* Fraser Forum 5, 9 (Feb. 1992).

[130]Dandridge v. Williams, 397 U.S. 471, 487 (1970).

[131]"The Federalist Papers" No. 78 at 465 (A. Hamilton) (A Mentor Book, 1961).

[132]Cutler and Schwartz, *supra* note 34 at 536.

[133]Adkins v. Children's Hospital, 261 U.S. 525, 561 (1923).

# Appendix I

# Suggested Model Constitution for Emerging Nations and Republics

### PREAMBLE
*(to be inserted)*

### ARTICLE I
*(Separation of Powers)*

The powers of the national government are legislative, executive, and judicial, and each is separate and distinct. Persons responsible for the exercise of one power may exercise either of the others only when permitted by this constitution.

### ARTICLE II
*(Structure and Procedures of National Assembly)*

*Section 1.* The National Assembly is the major legislative body of the Republic.

*Section 2.* The National Assembly shall consist of representatives who are elected from election districts of equal population. Each representative shall have one vote in the Assembly. Its members shall be elected by the people in universal, free, and secret elections at times and places and in a manner as prescribed by law.

*Section 3.* The National Assembly shall be elected every fourth year and hold office from the Monday after December 1 following the election until their successors qualify.

*Section 4.* Any person who has been a citizen of the Republic for at least five years, is 25 years of age or more, and has lived continuously in the district for at least one year is eligible for election as the district's representative to the National Assembly.

*Section 5.* To be elected to the National Assembly, a candidate must receive a majority of the votes in an initial or run-off election. If no candidate receives a majority in the first balloting, the two candidates receiving the highest number of the votes cast shall compete in a run-off election, to be held within two weeks thereafter. If either of the two run-off candidates is no longer willing or able to serve in the position, the candidate with the next highest vote in the initial balloting shall compete in the run-off election.

*Section 6.* (a) The National Assembly shall be the judge of the elections, returns, and qualifications of its own members, and a majority of the members shall constitute a quorum to do business. Decisions shall be made by majority vote except as otherwise herein provided.

(b) Except as otherwise herein provided, the Assembly shall determine its organization and the rules of its proceedings, punish its members for disorderly behavior, and, with the concurrence of two-thirds, expel a member.

(c) The Assembly shall keep a journal of its proceedings and votes, and from time to time publish the same, excepting such parts as may in its judgment require secrecy.

*Section 7.* The members of the Assembly shall receive a compensation for their services, to be provided by law, and paid out of the treasury of the Republic. They shall in all cases, except treason or felony, be privileged from arrest during their attendance at official sessions of the Assembly, and in going to and returning from the same. For their voting and statements in the Assembly, they shall bear no legal responsibility and shall otherwise not be questioned elsewhere. Members may not take other paid positions in the public or private sphere.

*Section 8.* No law shall be enacted except by introduction of a bill in the National Assembly, and prior to its passage, the following events occur:

(a) it has been referred to a committee, considered by such committee in session, and reported favorably;

(b) in the event the committee votes against the bill or takes no action within ___ days, a petition of discharge signed by ___ members of the Assembly shall have the same effect as a favorable committee vote;

(c) it has been printed and distributed to all members of the Assembly in the original or amended form at least two weeks prior to its being scheduled for vote;

(d) a vote is taken in which a majority of those present are recorded in the affirmative.

*Section 9.* To be a valid enactment of the National Assembly, each bill or constitutional amendment must not embrace more than one subject, which shall be expressed in its title. Appropriation bills shall concern only spending of monies and shall not mandate any other action or conduct. No bill except a general budget bill may contain more than one item of appropriation, and that for one expressed purpose.

*Section 10.* Before a bill passed by the National Assembly shall become law, it must be presented to the President of the Republic. If he approves he shall sign it, but if not he shall return it, with his objections to the National Assembly which may, if the objections are of constitutional nature, thereupon seek an opinion from the Constitutional Court as to its constitutionality. If the Court decides it is constitutional, or if the President's veto does not require a constitutional inquiry, and two-thirds of those voting in the Assembly shall agree to pass the bill, it shall become a Law. If any bill shall not be returned by the President within twelve days (Sundays excepted) after it shall have been presented to him, the same shall be a law, in like manner as if he had signed it, unless the National Assembly by their adjournment prevent its return, in which case it shall not be a law.

*Section 11.* The President shall have the power to reduce or eliminate one or more items of taxation or appropriation while approving other portions of a bill. In such cases, the President shall append to the bill a statement of the items reduced or eliminated with an explanation for the action, and transmit a copy of the bill and said statement to the Assembly within the 12-day period as provided previously. Items so reduced or eliminated shall be separately considered and may be passed over the President's veto by a two-thirds vote in the same manner as a bill.

*Section 12.* In addition to members of the Assembly, voters by petition shall have the right to initiate legislation in the National Assembly. Requirements for this procedure shall be prescribed by law.

## *ARTICLE III*
### *(Powers of the National Assembly)*

*Section 1.* (a) The authority of the National Assembly shall extend to all subjects of legislation not herein forbidden, restricted or otherwise constitutionally protected.

    (b) In addition, it shall have the power to ordain and establish

        (1) cabinet departments and administrative agencies to help execute the laws of the land. The highest officers of these bodies shall be nominated by the President and confirmed for office by a majority of the National Assembly. Any

department or agency so established shall have only such powers as are enumerated in the legislation creating it;

(2) regional governmental bodies to exercise enumerated legislative and executive powers at local geographical levels.

(c) It may vest the appointment of the ordinary officials of government in the President alone or in the Heads of Departments.

*Section 2.* Within the limitations imposed by this Constitution, the National Assembly shall in its best discretion and highest wisdom seek to improve and elevate the people's health, safety, well being and living conditions, advance and encourage education and culture, tax and spend for the common good and public interest, protect and preserve personal security and family life, enhance the environment, and safeguard the people from their domestic and foreign enemies.

*Section 3.* The National Assembly shall have no or limited powers in the following matters:

(a) The Assembly shall pass no law authorizing the national or any local government to purchase or own land or buildings except such as will be used solely for these purposes: public roads, public transportation, public sewers and water systems, public buildings, public schools, public parks, public hospitals and other public health facilities, and facilities for police, fire departments, and the armed forces, or any other absolutely essential public service. In the event the national or any local government seeks to purchase land or buildings for such purposes and the owner refuses to sell, a court may enter an order conveying the property to the government upon the latter paying the owner full market value for the asset and full compensation for any other economic loss sustained by the owner as a consequence of the government's action.

(b) Excepting that which it presently owns and operates, government shall not own or operate any commercial enterprise. Where government is presently engaged in commercial enterprise, freedom of entry into competing enterprises by private individuals or corporations shall not be restricted or prohibited.

(c) The Assembly shall not pass retroactive criminal or civil laws. This limitation shall not apply to civil legislation:

(1) enacted in conditions of emergency for the purpose of preserving law and order; provided, however, that such legislation shall be strictly limited to the extent and duration of the emergency;

(2)  prohibiting, regulating or abating without compensation, actions or uses damaging public health and safety or creating noxious conditions;

(3)  acquiring property and compensating owners therefor as permitted under this constitution; or

(4)  causing the value of property or of a commercial venture to be reduced less than ___ percent of its fair market value.

(d)  The powers of the National Assembly and any other governmental agency to lay and collect taxes, duties, imposts and excises, and spend monies are limited as follows:

(1)  The maximum amount of annual taxes on real property or on a commercial venture shall not exceed ___ percent of the full market value of such property or venture.

(2)  The total amount of taxes, duties, imposts, and excises collected in the country in any one year shall not exceed ___ percent of the gross national income of the nation for the prior year, except with the consent of two-thirds of the whole number of the National Assembly.

(3)  Neither the national government nor any local or regional government with taxing and spending powers shall incur an indebtedness or liability in any manner or for any purpose exceeding in any fiscal year the receipts to that government for that year, except with the consent of two-thirds of the whole number of the National Assembly.

(4)  When for any year, total receipts received by the Government exceeds total outlays, the surplus shall be used to reduce the amount levied for subsequent years.

(e)  The Assembly shall enact no law granting to any private group, corporation, association, union, or individual any special preference or exclusive right, privilege, or immunity.

(f)  The Assembly shall enact no law remitting, releasing, postponing, or diminishing any obligation or liability of any person, group, corporation, or association to the nation or to any political subdivision thereof.

(g)  The Assembly shall enact no law creating, increasing, or decreasing the salaries, fees, or allowances of public officers during the term for which they are elected or appointed. This limitation shall not apply to lifetime appointments. In the absence of substantial justification, the salary of an official appointed for life may at no time be reduced.

## ARTICLE IV
### (President)

*Section 1.* The President of the Republic of _____ is vested with the executive powers of the nation, and shall take care that the laws are faithfully executed.

*Section 2.* The President shall hold office for a term of 4 years and together with the Vice President shall be elected by the people in a universal, free, and secret election at times and places and in a manner as prescribed by law. The same person may not serve more than two consecutive terms in either office.

*Section 3.* (a) Any person born of _____ parentage who has attained the age of 40 years, and has resided continuously in _____ for at least ___ years is eligible for election as President or Vice President of the Republic.

(b) Candidates for President and Vice President shall run for office together on a ticket as a single choice for voters. For a president/vice president ticket to be certified for national election, a petition in its behalf containing ___ signatures of voters must be submitted as provided by law. The President and Vice President shall be elected every fourth year at the same time and places as members of the National Assembly and hold office from the Monday after January 1 following the election until their successors qualify.

(c) For candidates to be elected President and Vice President, their ticket must receive a majority of the votes in an initial or run-off election. If no ticket receives a majority in the first balloting, the two tickets receiving the highest number of the votes cast, shall compete in a run-off election, to be held within two weeks thereafter. If any candidate on the run-off tickets is no longer willing or able to serve in the designated office, the ticket with the next highest vote in the initial balloting shall compete in the run-off election.

*Section 4.* The President and Vice President shall receive compensation as provided by law, which may not be increased or decreased during their period of office.

*Section 5.* During the month of December following the election, the President shall form his Cabinet and submit it to the National Assembly for its consent by majority vote. If the National Assembly rejects individual members of the Cabinet, the President must submit replacement nominees until all members obtain the majority's approval.

*Section 6.* The President, Vice President, and other members of the cabinet may not take other paid positions in the public or private sphere.

*Section 7.* (a) If the President or Vice President engages in misconduct in office or high crimes, he may be impeached on a majority vote of the Assembly. The impeachment trial shall be public and held by the Assembly in its chambers. The Chief Justice of the Constitutional Court shall preside and a conviction shall require a two-thirds vote of the whole number of the Assembly.

(b) Judgment in impeachment may extend only to removal from office and disqualification to hold any office in the Republic, but the person convicted or acquitted shall remain subject to criminal punishment according to law.

*Section 8.* In addition to exercising the powers heretofore set forth, the President of the Republic shall

(a) from time to time report to the National Assembly on the condition of the Republic, and recommend to its consideration such measures as he shall deem necessary and expedient.

(b) submit annually a budget for the Republic to the National Assembly for its review and confirmation; and submit periodically an accounting to the National Assembly and to the people concerning government expenditures and receipts and the financial state of the Republic;

(c) convene the National Assembly when it is not in session.

(d) represent the Republic in international relationships;

(e) conclude and execute international treaties and other agreements, which are subject to ratification by the National Assembly;

(f) appoint certain judges of the Supreme Court;

(g) appoint ministers of the cabinet, ambassadors, consuls, and trade representatives of the Republic, with the consent of the National Assembly;

(h) relate and communicate with leaders of other States on matters of international relations, and name representatives to conduct such negotiations;

(i) be the Commander-in-Chief of the Armed Forces, and appoint and retire the highest levels of military commanders with the approval of the National Assembly;

(j) declare, when necessary, emergency conditions throughout the Republic, or in specific regions, which will require confirmation by the National Assembly, within five days;

(k) arrange for either partial or general mobilization of the Armed Forces with previous approval of National Assembly; in an emergency or when there is a threat of attack on the Republic, such action requiring confirmation by the National Assembly within five days thereafter;

(l)   order the start of military hostilities in the event of an attack on the Republic, which will require confirmation by the National Assembly within five days;

(m)   exercise the right of pardon throughout the Republic, except in cases of impeachment, all in accordance with law;

(n)   grant honor medals and other awards of the Republic of _____, and confer honorary titles.

*Section 9.* In case of the removal of the President from office, or of his death, resignation, or inability to discharge the duties of the office, the same shall devolve on the vice president, and the Assembly shall by law provide for the case of removal, death, resignation or inability, both of the President and Vice President until such time as a new President and Vice President are elected.

## ARTICLE V
### (Judiciary)

*Section 1.* The judicial power of this nation shall be vested in one Supreme Court and in such inferior courts as the National Assembly shall from time to time ordain and establish. The organization and procedures of the Supreme and inferior courts shall be established by the National Assembly.

*Section 2.* The judicial power shall extend to all cases arising under this Constitution and the laws and treaties of the Republic, and to controversies involving or affecting persons, corporations, associations, organizations, and political bodies and agencies located within the territorial boundaries of the Republic.

*Section 3.* The Supreme Court shall consist of two branches, one branch to be known as the Constitutional Court, and to decide exclusively matters requiring interpretation of the constitution. The other branch shall be known as the Supreme Judicial Court and shall be a tribunal of final appeal on all other judicial matters, both as to law and fact, except it shall have original jurisdiction in emergency matters.

*Section 4.* The Constitutional Court is a court of original and final jurisdiction and shall protect the powers, structure and organization of government, and the liberties of the people, as provided and required under the terms and provisions of this constitution. It shall entertain and decide complaints of unconstitutionality filed by any government agency, government official, person, domestic corporation or foreign corporation adversely affected by alleged unconstitutional action.

*Section 5.* Once its jurisdiction has been invoked, the Constitutional Court shall have the power to invalidate any law, ordinance, or regulation that violates this Constitution, whether adopted by the legislature or imposed by the President or by any governmental body or agency. It shall also have the power to mandate the government to fully compensate persons or corporations whose constitutional rights have been violated for the damages they have sustained. It shall issue constitutional advisory opinions to the National Assembly when the President vetoes a measure on a constitutional basis but not otherwise.

*Section 6.* The Constitutional Court shall consist of nine members, four appointed by the National Assembly, and five by the President of the Republic, and their term of office shall be for life, except as otherwise herein provided. The President shall appoint the Chief Justice.

*Section 7.* The Constitutional Court shall have solely negative power in enforcing the Constitution. Except with respect to compensating persons as aforesaid, it may do no more than invalidate laws, ordinances, and regulations. It shall have no power to impose laws, ordinances, or regulations or direct the Assembly, President, or any government agencies to impose laws, ordinances, or regulations. It shall not monitor these other branches in the execution of their functions except when they usurp constitutional powers or deny or deprive persons or corporations of protected liberties.

*Section 8.* Judges shall not apply laws that are inconsistent with the Constitution. In the event that in the course of a judicial proceeding a court determines that it must apply a law that might violate the constitution, the court shall adjourn the proceeding and make a formal request for a decision by the Constitutional Court on the constitutionality of the law. If the law is found valid, the original proceeding shall continue.

*Section 9.* (a) The Supreme Judicial Court of the Republic shall consist of nine justices, three to be elected as provided by law, three to be appointed by the National Assembly and three to be appointed by the President of the Republic. The President shall appoint the Chief Justice.

(b) Members of the Supreme Judicial Court serve in their office until the age of retirement, as specified by law, and except as otherwise herein provided.

*Section 10.* During their term in office, Supreme Court Justices are subject to dismissal only for misconduct in office or high crimes to be determined in a proceeding for impeachment. The proceedings shall be the same as set forth heretofore for impeachment of executive officers. If the Chief Justice of the Constitutional Court is impeached, the most senior of the remaining justices of the Constitutional Court shall preside.

## ARTICLE VI
### (Personal Rights)

*Section 1.* The Republic of _____ is a free nation dedicated to preserving, protecting and encouraging freedom within its territorial boundaries. No liberties are absolute but may be limited only pursuant to the terms and provisions of this Constitution.

*Section 2.* All persons permanently residing within the geographical borders of the Republic are citizens. At the age of eighteen or more a citizen who is otherwise qualified by law may register and vote.

*Section 3.* Every citizen has the right of peaceful and nonviolent assembly and of petition for any matter.

*Section 4.* Every citizen has the right, either alone or jointly with others, privately or in public, to practice and profess any religious or atheistic faith, dogma, or beliefs.

*Section 5.* Every citizen and domestic corporation has the right to express and disseminate information, opinions, and beliefs by word, writing or picture.

*Section 6.* Every citizen has the right of academic freedom and research and to engage in the arts.

*Section 7.* Every citizen and domestic corporation has the right to receive, gather, and have access to obtain information and ideas.

*Section 8.* Every citizen is equal before the procedures and processes of the law.

*Section 9.* Every citizen has the right of residence and movement throughout the nation and to a foreign country.

*Section 10.* Every citizen and corporation has a right to secrecy in personal correspondence and communication, whether by post, telephone, telegraph, or other such facilities.

*Section 11.* Individuals and corporations who cause injury to person or property shall be immune from criminal or tort liability for that injury if when causing it they obeyed the relevant laws, and did not act negligently.

*Section 12.* Every citizen and domestic corporation has the right to purchase, acquire, rent, own, use, mortgage, sell, lease, transfer, bequeath and inherit private property, or any part or portion thereof. Private property includes any asset or thing of value, whether tangible or intangible, real or personal.

*Section 13.* Every citizen and domestic corporation has the right freely to practice the occupation, profession, or trade of choice, freely to establish and maintain a commercial enterprise, and freely to produce and distribute goods and services.

*Section 14.* Every citizen and domestic corporation has the right to enter into binding agreements containing any and only provisions of their choice.

*Section 15.* Every citizen has the right of free association, and to join with others and form corporations, associations, unions and any other organizations as long as the objective is peaceful and nonviolent.

*Section 16.* In addition to the rights enumerated in this Constitution, the Constitutional Court shall have the power to determine and protect unenumerated rights, according to the principles which follow.

*Section 17.* (a) No governmental entity shall deprive any person of the rights herein enumerated or of other rights of life, liberty, or property not enumerated except first, as a sanction for the commission of criminal or civil wrongdoing, and second, when a deprivation is necessary for the National Assembly or an executive authority to effectuate constitutional powers as herein set forth.

(b) The rights of "life, liberty, and property" include any form of human activity that is not destructive of the rights of life, liberty, and property of others, and applies to all persons at and above the age of 18 and corporations. The terms "life, liberty and property" comprehend only self-inspired or self-initiated actions and not liberties, rights, privileges, positions, immunities, entitlements, or subsidies created by the political process.

*Section 18.* All rights and freedoms provided by this Constitution are guaranteed to foreign nationals and persons without citizenship residing within the territory of this nation.

*Section 19.* The government has no constitutional obligation to support, advance or otherwise subsidize any private activities, even when the absence of funds may limit the enjoyment of protected rights.

*Section 20.* In deciding whether the denial or deprivation of a protected right by the Assembly or an executive authority is valid under the constitution, the Constitutional Court shall require that the governmental authority prove the existence of each of the following four conditions:

(a) The objective of the law or regulation is within the power of the government body that adopted it.

(b) The law or regulation is within the power of the government body that adopted it and is substantially related to the achievement of this objective, that is, the means is legitimate and the fit between it and the ends is close.

(c) There is a proportionality between the effects of the restraint and its objective, that is, the consequences of the restraint are not out of proportion to its benefits. The more severe the deleterious effects of a measure, the more societally important the objective must be.

(d) The same objective cannot be achieved by a law less harmful to the exercise of liberty. To be acceptable the law utilized should impair liberty to the least degree possible, that is, no less onerous and feasible alternative legislative solution exists.

If the government proves each of the foregoing conditions, under the ordinary standard of proof in civil litigation, the Court shall sustain the law or regulation in issue.

## ARTICLE VII
### (Protection of Accused Persons)

*Section 1.* The criminal system must never be used to punish persons innocent of wrongdoing. It must also never shield from punishment the perpetrators of crimes. Legal violations or errors committed by the police or the prosecutor in the enforcement of the criminal code shall not preclude a judge or other the trier of fact from determining guilt of an accused. No person shall be arrested or detained by government except pursuant to the processes herein set forth.

*Section 2.* Police may not hold anyone in custody on their own authority longer than the end of the day after the day of apprehension. Only a judge so authorized may order detention subsequent to this time, and for the period pending disposition by a trial. Detained persons shall not be subjected to mental or physical mistreatment. No one shall be detained without adequate cause. Persons convicted of crime shall not be subject to cruel and unusual punishments or excessive fines.

*Section 3.* (a) An accused person may be released on bail by sufficient monetary guarantees, except for capital crimes when the facts are strong for conviction. In setting, reducing, or denying bail, the judge shall take into consideration primarily the protection of the public. In addition, the seriousness of the offense charged, the previous criminal record of the accused, and the probability of his or her appearing at the trial or hearing of the case should also be considered. The amount of bail shall not be excessive.

(b) Before any person arrested for a serious felony may be released on bail, a hearing shall be held by a judge, and the attorney for the government shall be given opportunity to be heard in the matter.

*Section 4.* The imposition of penalties and punishment shall be solely the responsibility of the judiciary, and the legislature shall have no authority in this regard except to enumerate and proscribe sentences for criminal wrongdoing. Nor shall the legislature avoid the protections provided herein by labelling punishments as civil penalties.

*Section 5.* At every stage of criminal process, an accused shall be entitled to being informed of the charges against him or her, and, if appropriate, to a hearing which gives him or her full opportunity to present a defense. He or she shall be entitled to the privilege of counsel at all times, which shall be provided by the government at its expense when the accused cannot afford payment for such services. An accused who does not speak the language in which the proceedings are conducted shall be provided without expense the services of an interpreter.

*Section 6.* An accused shall be presumed innocent until proven guilty in a fair and public hearing by an independent and impartial tribunal; he or she shall enjoy the right to a speedy and public trial; he or she shall be permitted full opportunity to examine all witnesses, and he or she shall have the right of compulsory process for obtaining witnesses on their behalf at public expense; he or she shall not be compelled to testify against themselves or be forced to confess under compulsion, torture or threat or after prolonged detention in prison; and he or she shall not be tried more than once for the same crime.

*Section 7.* The right of all persons to be secure in their homes, papers and effects against entries, searches and seizures shall not be impaired except upon warrant issued by a judge for adequate cause and particularly describing the place to be searched and the persons or things to be seized. However, in the event of danger in delay, these powers may be exercised as provided by the National Assembly.

*Section 8.* A person who has been illegally arrested, detained, or imprisoned may receive indemnity for physical injury or material losses suffered thereby.

*Section 9.* As part of the sentence imposed for criminal wrongdoing, judges shall require restitution from the convicted person to a crime victim who suffers a loss, unless compelling and extraordinary reasons exist to the contrary.

## *ARTICLE VIII*
### *(National Concerns Symbols and Language)*

*Section 1.* The official language of the Republic is _____. Education and business shall be conducted in _____, except as provided by law.

*Section 2.* The national symbols of the Republic are the following:

The flag is ....

The national hymn is ....

The national Coat of Arms is ....

*Section 3.* The Capital of the Republic is _____.

*Section 4.* No person holding a paid position in the government of the Republic may receive from any other nation or one of its officials any gift, award, or grant without approval of the National Assembly.

## *ARTICLE IX*
### *(Ratification of Constitution and Amendments)*

*Section 1.* This Constitution shall not be binding on the People of _____ unless and until (1) two-thirds of the whole number of the National Assembly shall vote for its adoption and (2) soon thereafter more than 50% of the people eligible to vote shall vote in its favor.

*Section 2.* This Constitution may be amended only by successful completion of the following requirements:

(a) every amendment must be initially adopted by a two-third's vote of the whole number of the National Assembly;

(b) after the Assembly adopts the proposed amendment as aforesaid, it must within two months thereafter schedule a public vote on the amendment; and

(c) to be ratified and binding, a majority of those persons eligible to vote must vote for the amendment.

*Section 3.* Constitutional amendments do not require approval of the President.

### *END OF SUGGESTED MODEL*

# Appendix II

# The Constitution of the United States of America

We the People of the United States, in Order to form a more perfect Union, establish Justice, insure domestic Tranquility, provide for the common defence, promote the general Welfare, and secure the Blessings of Liberty to ourselves and our Posterity, do ordain and establish this Constitution for the United States of America.

## ARTICLE I

*Section 1.* All legislative Powers herein granted shall be vested in a Congress of the United States, which shall consist of a Senate and House of Representatives.

*Section 2.* The House of Representatives shall be composed of Members chosen every second Year by the People of the several States, and the Electors in each State shall have the Qualifications requisite for Electors of the most numerous Branch of the State Legislature.

No Person shall be a Representative who shall not have attained to the Age of twenty-five Years, and been seven Years a Citizen of the United States, and who shall not, when elected, be an Inhabitant of that State in which he shall be chosen.

Representatives and direct Taxes shall be apportioned among the several States which may be included within this Union, according to their respective Numbers, which shall be determined by adding to the whole Number of free Persons, including those bound to Service for a Term of Years, and excluding Indians not taxed, three fifths of all other Persons. The actual Enumeration shall be made within three Years after the first Meeting of the Congress of the United States, and within every subsequent Term of ten Years, in such Manner as they shall by Law direct. The Number of Representatives shall not exceed one for every thirty Thousand, but each State shall have at Least one Representative; and until such enumerations shall to be made, the State of New Hampshire shall be entitled to chuse three, Massachusetts eight, Rhode-Island and Providence Plantations one, Connecticut five, New-York six, New Jersey four, Pennsylvania eight, Delaware one, Maryland six, Virginia ten, North Carolina five, South Carolina five, and Georgia three.

When vacancies happen in the Representation from any State, the Executive Authority thereof shall issue Writs of Election to fill such Vacancies.

The House of Representatives shall chuse their Speaker and other Officers; and shall have the sole Power of Impeachment.

*Section 3.* The Senate of the United States shall be composed of two Senators from each State, chosen by the Legislature thereof, for six Years; and each Senator shall have one Vote.

Immediately after they shall be assembled in Consequence of the first Election, they shall be divided as equally as may be into three Classes. The Seats of the Senators of the first Class shall be vacated at the Expiration of Seats of the second Year, of the second Class at the Expiration of the fourth Year, and of the third Class at the Expiration of the sixth Year, so that one-third may be chosen every second Year; and if Vacancies happen by Resignation, or otherwise, during the Recess of the Legislature of any State, the Executive thereof may make temporary Appointments until the next Meeting of the Legislature, which shall then fill such Vacancies.

No Person shall be a Senator who shall not have attained to the Age of thirty Years, and been nine Years a Citizen of the United States, and who shall not, when elected, be an Inhabitant of that State for which he shall be chosen.

The Vice President of the United States shall be President of the Senate, but shall have no Vote, unless they be equally divided.

The Senate shall chuse their other Officers, and also a President pro tempore, in the absence of the Vice President, or when he shall exercise the Office of President of the United States.

The Senate shall have the sole Power to try all Impeachments. When sitting for that Purpose, they shall be on Oath or Affirmation. When the President of the United States is tried, the Chief Justice shall preside: And no Person shall be convicted without the concurrence of two thirds of the Members present.

Judgment in Cases of Impeachment shall not extend further than to removal from Office, and disqualification to hold and enjoy any Office of honor, Trust or Profit under the United States: but the Party convicted shall nevertheless be liable and subject to Indictment, Trial, Judgment and Punishment, according to Law.

*Section 4.* The Times, Places and Manner of holding Elections for Senators and Representatives, shall be prescribed in each State by the Legislature thereof; but the Congress may at any time by Law make or alter such Regulations, except as to the Place of Chusing Senators.

The Congress shall assemble at least once every Year, and such Meeting shall be on the first Monday in December, unless they shall by Law appoint a different Day.

*Section 5.* Each House shall be the Judge of the Elections, Returns and Qualifications of its own Members, and a Majority of each shall constitute a Quorum to do Business; but a smaller number may adjourn from day to day, and may be authorized to compel the Attendance of absent Members, in such Manner, and under such Penalties as each House may provide.

Each House may determine the Rules of its Proceedings, punish its Members for disorderly Behavior, and, with the Concurrence of two thirds, expel a Member.

Each House shall keep a Journal of its Proceedings, and from time to time publish the same, excepting such Parts as may in their Judgment require Secrecy; and the Yeas and Nays of the Members of either House on any question shall, at the Desire of one fifth of those Present, be entered on the Journal.

Neither House, during the Session of Congress, shall, without the Consent of the other, adjourn for more than three days, nor to any other Place than that in which the two Houses shall be sitting.

*Section 6.* The Senators and Representatives shall receive a Compensation for their Services, to be ascertained by Law, and paid out of the Treasury of the United States. They shall in all Cases, except Treason, Felony and Breach of the Peace, be privileged from Arrest during their Attendance of the Session of their respective Houses, and in going to and returning from the same; and for any Speech or Debate in either House, they shall not be questioned in any other Place.

No Senator or Representative shall, during the Time for which he was elected, be appointed to any civil Office under the Authority of the United States, which shall have been created, or the Emoluments whereof shall have been encreased during such time; and no Person holding any Office under the United States, shall be a Member of either House during his Continuance in Office.

*Section 7.* All Bills for raising Revenue shall originate in the House of Representatives; but the Senate may propose or concur with Amendments as on other Bills.

Every Bill which shall have passed the House of Representatives and the Senate, shall, before it become a Law, be presented to the President of the United States; If he approve he shall sign it, but if not he shall return it, with his Objections to that House in which it shall have originated, who shall enter the Objections at large on their Journal, and proceed to reconsider it. If after such Reconsideration two thirds of that House shall agree to pass the Bill, it shall be sent, together with the Objections to the other House, by which it shall likewise be reconsidered, and if approved by two thirds of that House, it shall become a Law. But in all such Cases the Votes of both Houses shall be determined by Yeas and Nays, and the Names of the Persons voting for and against the Bill shall be entered on the Journal of each House respectively. If any Bill shall not be returned by the President within ten Days (Sunday excepted) after it shall have been presented to him, the Same shall be a Law, in like manner as if he had signed it, unless the Congress by their Adjournment prevent its Return, in which Case it shall not be a Law.

Every Order, Resolution, or Vote to which the Concurrence of the Senate and the House of Representatives may be necessary (except on a question of Adjournment) shall be presented to the President of the United States; and before the Same shall take Effect, shall be approved by him, or being disapproved by him, shall be repassed by two thirds of the Senate and House of Representatives, according to the Rules and Limitations prescribed in the Case of a Bill.

*Section 8.* The Congress shall have Power To lay and collect Taxes, Duties, Imposts and Excises, to pay the Debts and provide for the common Defense and general Welfare of the United States; but all Duties, Imposts and Excises shall be uniform throughout the United States;

To borrow money on the credit of the United States;

To regulate Commerce with foreign Nations, and among the several States, and with Indian Tribes;

To establish an uniform Rule of Naturalization and uniform Laws on the subject of Bankruptcies throughout the United States;

To coin Money, regulate the Value thereof, and of foreign Coin, and fix the Standard of Weights and Measures;

To provide for the Punishment of counterfeiting the Securities and current Coin of the United States;

To establish Post Offices and post Roads;

To promote the Progress of Science and useful Arts, by securing for limited Times to Authors and Investors the exclusive Right to their respective Writings and Discoveries;

To constitute Tribunals inferior to the Supreme Court;

To define and punish Piracies and Felonies committed on the high Seas, and Offenses against the Law of Nations;

To declare War, grant Letters of Marque and Reprisal, and make Rules concerning Captures on Land and Water;

To raise and support Armies, but no Appropriation of Money to that Use shall be for a longer Term than two Years;

To provide and maintain a Navy;

To make Rules for the Government and Regulation of the land and naval Forces;

To provide for calling for the Militia to execute the Laws of the Union, suppress Insurrections and repel Invasions;

To provide for organizing, arming, and disciplining the Militia, and for governing such Part of them as may be employed in the Service of the United States, reserving to the States respectively, the Appointment of the Officers, and the Authority of training the Militia according to the discipline prescribed by Congress;

To exercise exclusive Legislation in all Cases whatsoever, over such District (not exceeding ten Miles square) as may, by Cession of particular States, and the acceptance of Congress, become the Seat of the Government of the United States, and to exercise like Authority over all Places purchased by the Consent of the Legislature of the State in which the Same shall be, for the Erection of Forts, Magazines, Arsenals, dock-Yards, and other needful Buildings;—And

To make all Laws which shall be necessary and proper for carrying into Execution the foregoing Powers, and all other Powers vested by this Constitution in the Government of the United States, or in any Department or Officer thereof.

*Section 9.* The Migration or Importation of such Persons as any of the States now existing shall think proper to admit, shall not be prohibited by the Congress prior to the Year one thousand eight hundred and eight, but a tax or duty may be imposed on such Importation, not exceeding ten dollars for each Person.

The privilege of the Writ of Habeas Corpus shall not be suspended, unless when in Cases of Rebellion or Invasion the public Safety may require it.

No Bill of Attainder or ex post facto Law shall be passed.

No capitation, or other direct, Tax shall be laid, unless in Proportion to the Census or Enumeration herein before directed to be taken.

No Tax or Duty shall be laid on Articles exported from any State.

No Preference shall be given by any Regulation of Commerce or Revenue to the Ports of one State over those of another: nor shall Vessels bound to, or from, one State, be obliged to enter, clear, or pay Duties in another.

No Money shall be drawn from the Treasury, but in Consequence of Appropriations made by Law; and a regular Statement and Account of the Receipts and Expenditures of all public Money shall be published from time to time.

No title of Nobility shall be granted by the United States: And no Person holding any Office of Profit or Trust under them, shall, without the Consent of the Congress, accept of any present, Emolument, Office, or Title, of any kind whatever, from any King, Prince, or foreign State.

*Section 10.* No State shall enter into any Treaty, Alliance, or Confederation; grant Letters of Marque and Reprisal; coin Money; emit Bills of Credit; make any Thing but gold and silver Coin a Tender in Payment of Debts; pass any Bill of Attainder, ex post facto Law, or Law impairing the Obligation of Contracts, or grant any title of Nobility.

No State shall, without the Consent of the Congress, lay any Imposts or Duties on Imports or Exports, except what may be absolutely necessary for executing its inspection Laws: and the net Produce of all Duties and Imposts, laid by any State on Imports or Exports, shall be for the Use of the Treasury of the United States; and all such Laws shall be subject to the Revision and Controul of the Congress.

No State shall, without the consent of Congress, lay any duty of tonnage, keep Troops, or Ships of War in time of Peace, enter into any Agreement or Compact with another State, or with a foreign Power, or engage in War, unless actually invaded, or in such imminent Danger as will not admit of delay.

## ARTICLE II

*Section 1.* The executive Power shall be vested in a President of the United States of America. He shall hold his Office during the Term of four Years, and, together with the Vice-President, chosen for the same Term be elected as follows.

Each State shall appoint, in such Manner as the Legislature thereof may direct, a Number of Electors, equal to the whole Number of Senators and Representatives to which the State may be entitled in the Congress: but no Senator or Representative, or Person holding an Office of Trust or Profit under the United States, shall be appointed an Elector.

The Electors shall meet in their respective States, and vote by Ballot for two persons, of whom one at least shall not be an Inhabitant of the same State with themselves. And they shall make a List of all the Persons voted for, and of the Number of Votes for each; which List they shall sign and certify, and transmit sealed to the Seat of the Government of the United States, directed to the President of the Senate. The President of the Senate shall, in the Presence of the Senate and House of Representatives, open all the Certificates, and the Votes shall then be counted. The Person having the greatest Number of Votes shall be the President, if such Number be a Majority of the whole Number of Electors appointed; and if there be more than one who have such Majority, and have an equal Number of Votes, then the House of Representatives shall immediately chuse by Ballot one of them for President; and if no Person have a Majority, then from the five highest on the List the said House shall in like Manner chuse the President. But in chusing the President, the Votes shall be taken by States, the Representation from each State having one Vote; a quorum for this Purpose shall consist of a Member of Members from two thirds of the States, and a Majority of all the States shall be necessary to a Choice. In every Case, after the Choice of the President, the Person having the greatest Number of Votes of the Electors shall be the Vice President. But if there should remain two or more who have equal Votes, the Senate shall chuse from them by Ballot the Vice President.

The Congress may determine the Time of chusing the Electors, and the Day on which they shall give their Votes; which Day shall be the same throughout the United States.

No Person except a natural born Citizen, or a Citizen of the United States, at the time of the Adoption of this Constitution, shall be eligible to the Office of President; neither shall any Person be eligible to that Office who shall not have attained to the Age of thirty-five Years, and been fourteen Years a Resident within the United States.

In Case of the Removal of the President from Office, or of his Death, Resignation, or Inability to discharge the Powers and Duties of the said Office, the same shall devolve on the Vice President, and the Congress may by Law, provide for the Case of Removal, Death Resignation or Inability, both of the President and Vice President, declaring what Officer shall then act as President, and such Officer shall act accordingly, until the Disability be removed, or a President shall be elected.

The President shall, at stated Times, receive for his Services, a Compensation, which shall neither be encreased nor diminished during the Period for which he shall have been elected, and he shall not receive within that Period any other Emolument from the United States, or any of them.

Before he enter on the Execution of his Office, he shall take the following Oath or Affirmation:—"I do solemnly swear (or affirm) that I will faithfully execute the Office of President of the United States, and will to the best of my Ability, preserve, protect and defend the Constitution of the United States."

*Section 2.* The President shall be Commander in Chief of the Army and Navy of the United States, and of the Militia of the several States, when called into the actual Service of the United States; he may require the Opinion in writing, of the principal Officer in each of the executive Departments, upon any subject relating to the Duties of their respective Offices, and he shall have Power to Grant Reprieves and Pardons for Offenses against the United States, except in Cases of Impeachment.

He shall have Power, by and with the Advice and Consent of the Senate, to make Treaties, provided two-thirds of the Senators present concur; and he shall nominate, and by and with the Advice and Consent of the Senate, shall appoint Ambassadors, other public ministers and Consuls, Judges of the supreme Court, and all other Officers of the United States, whose Appointments are not herein otherwise provided for, and which shall be established by Law; but the Congress may by Law vest the Appointment of such inferior Officers, as they think proper, in the President alone, in the Courts of Law, or in the Heads of Departments.

The President shall have Power to fill up all Vacancies that may happen during the Recess of the Senate, by granting Commissions which shall expire at the End of their next Session.

*Section 3.* He shall from time to time give to the Congress Information of the State of the Union, and recommend to their Consideration such Measures as he shall judge necessary and expedient; he may, on extraordinary Occasions, convene both Houses, or either of them, and in Case of Disagreement between them, with Respect to the Time of Adjournment, he may adjourn them to such Time as he shall think proper; he shall receive Ambassadors and other public Ministers; he shall take Care that the Laws be faithfully executed, and shall Commission all the Officers of the United States.

*Section 4.* The President, Vice President and all Civil Officers of the United States, shall be removed from Office on Impeachment for, and Conviction of, Treason, Bribery, or other high Crimes, and Misdemeanors.

## ARTICLE III

*Section 1.* The judicial Power of the United States, shall be vested in one supreme Court, and in such inferior Courts as the Congress may from time to time ordain and establish. The Judges, both of the supreme and inferior Courts, shall hold their Offices during good Behavior, and shall, at stated Times, receive for their Services, a Compensation, which shall not be diminished during their Continuance in Office.

*Section 2.* The judicial Power shall extend to all Cases, in Law and Equity, arising under this Constitution, the Laws of the United States, and Treaties made, or which shall be made, under their Authority;—to all Cases affecting Ambassadors, other public Ministers and Consuls;—to all Cases of admiralty and maritime Jurisdiction;—to Controversies to which the United States shall be a Party;—to Controversies between two or more States;—between a State and Citizens of another State;—between Citizens of different States;—between Citizens of the same State claiming Lands under Grants of different States, and between a State, or the Citizens thereof, and foreign States, Citizens or Subjects.

In all Cases affecting Ambassadors, other public Ministers and Consuls, and those in which a State shall be Party, the supreme Court shall have original Jurisdiction. In all the other cases before mentioned, the supreme Court shall have appellate Jurisdiction, both as to Law and Fact, with such Exceptions, and under such Regulations as the Congress shall make.

The trial of all Crimes, except in Cases of Impeachment, shall be by Jury; and such Trial shall be held in the State where the said Crimes shall have been committed; but when not committed within any State, the Trial shall be at such Place or Places as the Congress may by Law have directed.

*Section 3.* Treason against the United States, shall consist only in levying War against them, or in adhering to their Enemies, giving them Aid and Comfort. No Person shall be convicted of Treason unless on the Testimony of two Witnesses to the same overt Act, or on Confession in open Court.

The Congress shall have Power to declare the Punishment of Treason, but no Attainder of Treason shall work Corruption of Blood, or Forfeiture except during the Life of the Person attainted.

## ARTICLE IV

*Section 1.* Full Faith and Credit shall be given in each State to the public Acts, Records, and judicial Proceedings of every other State. And the Congress may by general Laws prescribe the Manner in which such Acts, Records and Proceedings shall be proved, and the Effect thereof.

*Section 2.* The Citizens of each State shall be entitled to all Privileges and Immunities of Citizens in the several States.

A Person charged in any State with Treason, Felony, or other Crime, who shall flee from Justice, and be found in another State, shall on demand of the executive Authority of the State from which he fled, be delivered up, to be removed to the State having Jurisdiction of the Crime.

No Person held to Service or Labour in one State, under the Laws thereof, escaping into another, shall, in Consequence of any Law or Regulation therein, be discharged from such Service or Labour, but shall be delivered up on Claim of the Party to whom such Service or Labour may be due.

*Section 3.* New States may be admitted by the Congress into this Union; but no new State shall be formed or erected within the Jurisdiction of any other State; nor any State be formed by the Junction of two or more States, or parts of States, without the Consent of the Legislatures of the States concerned as well as of the Congress.

The Congress shall have Power to dispose of and make all needful Rules and Regulations respecting the Territory or other Property belonging to the United States; and nothing in this Constitution shall be so construed as to Prejudice any Claims of the United States, or of any particular State.

*Section 4.* The United States shall guarantee to every State in this Union a Republican Form of Government, and shall protect each of them against Invasion; and on Application of the Legislature, or of the Executive (when the Legislature cannot be convened) against domestic Violence.

## *ARTICLE V*

The Congress, whenever two-thirds of both Houses shall deem it necessary, shall propose Amendments to this Constitution, or, on the Application of the Legislatures of two-thirds of the several States, shall call a Convention for proposing Amendments, which, in either Case, shall be valid to all Intents and Purposes, as part of this Constitution, when ratified by the Legislatures of three-fourths of the several States, or by Conventions in three-fourths thereof, as the one or the other Mode of Ratification may be proposed by the Congress: Provided that no Amendment which may be made prior to the Year One thousand eight hundred and eight shall in any Manner affect the first and fourth Clauses in the Ninth Section of the first Article; and that no State without its Consent, shall be deprived of its equal Suffrage in the Senate.

## ARTICLE VI

All Debts contracted and Engagements entered into, before the Adoption of this Constitution, shall be as valid against the United States under this Constitution, as under the Confederation.

This Constitution, and the Laws of the United States which shall be made in Pursuance thereof; and all Treaties made, or which shall be made, under the Authority of the United States, shall be the supreme Law of the Land, and the Judges in every State shall be bound thereby, any Thing in the Constitution or Laws of any State to the contrary notwithstanding.

The Senators and Representatives before mentioned, and the Members of the several State Legislatures, and all executive and judicial Officers, both of the United States and of the several States, shall be bound by Oath or Affirmation, to support this Constitution; but no religious Test shall ever be required as a Qualification to any Office or public Trust under the United States.

## ARTICLE VII

The Ratification of the Conventions of nine States shall be sufficient for the Establishment of this Constitution between the States so ratifying the Same.

Done in Convention by the Unanimous Consent of the States present the Seventeenth Day of September in the Year of Our Lord one thousand seven hundred and Eighty seven and of the Independence of the United States of America the Twelfth.

In Witness whereof We have hereunto subscribed our Names.

### AMENDMENT I

Congress shall make no law respecting an establishment of religion, or prohibiting the free exercise thereof; or abridging the freedom of speech, or of the press; or the right of the people peaceably to assemble, and to petition the Government for a redress of grievances.

### AMENDMENT II

A well regulated Militia, being necessary to the security of a free State, the right of the people to keep and bear Arms, shall not be infringed.

### AMENDMENT III

No Soldier shall, in time of peace be quartered in any house, without the consent of the Owner, nor in time of war, but in a manner to be prescribed by law.

*AMENDMENT IV*

The right of the people to be secure in their persons, houses, papers, and effects, against unreasonable searches and seizures, shall not be violated, and no Warrants shall issue, but upon probable cause, supported by Oath or affirmation, and particularly describing the place to be searched, and the persons or things to be seized.

*AMENDMENT V*

No person shall be held to answer for a capital, or otherwise infamous crime, unless on presentment or indictment of a Grand Jury, except in cases arising in the land or naval forces, or in the Militia, when in actual service in time of War or public danger; nor shall any person be subject for the same offence to be twice put in jeopardy of life or limb; nor shall be compelled in any criminal case to be a witness against himself, nor be deprived of life, liberty, or property, without due process of law; nor shall private property be taken for public use, without just compensation.

*AMENDMENT VI*

In all criminal prosecutions, the accused shall enjoy the right to a speedy and public trial, by an impartial jury of the State and district wherein the crime shall have been committed, which district shall have been previously ascertained by law, and to be informed of the nature and cause of the accusation; to be confronted with the witness against him; to have compulsory process for obtaining witnesses in his favor, and to have the Assistance of Counsel for his defence.

*AMENDMENT VII*

In suits at common law, where the value in controversy shall exceed twenty dollars, the right of trial by jury shall be preserved, and no fact tried by a jury, shall be otherwise reexamined in any Court of the United States, than according to the rules of the common law.

*AMENDMENT VIII*

Excessive bail shall not be required, nor excessive fines imposed, nor cruel and unusual punishments inflicted.

*AMENDMENT IX*

The enumeration in the Constitution, of certain rights, shall not be construed to deny or disparage others retained by the people.

*AMENDMENT X*

The powers not delegated to the United States by the Constitution, nor prohibited by it to the States, are reserved to the States respectively, or to the people.

*AMENDMENT XI*

The Judicial power of the United States shall not be construed to extend to any suit in law or equity, commenced or prosecuted against one of the United States by Citizens of another State, or by Citizens or Subjects of any Foreign State.

*AMENDMENT XII*

The Electors shall meet in their respective states and vote by ballot for President and Vice-President, one of whom, at least, shall not be an inhabitant of the same state with themselves; they shall name in their ballots the person voted for as President, and in distinct ballots the persons voted for as Vice-President, and they shall make distinct lists of all persons voted for as President, and of all persons voted for as Vice-President, and the number of votes for each, which lists they shall sign and certify, and transmit sealed to the seat of the government of the United States, directed to the President of the Senate;—The President of the Senate shall, in presence of the Senate and House of Representatives, open all the certificates and the votes shall then be counted;—The person having the greatest number of votes for President, shall be the President, if such number be a majority of the whole number of Electors appointed; and if no person have such majority, then from the persons having the highest numbers not exceeding three on the list of those voted for as President, the House of Representatives shall choose immediately, by ballot, the President. But in choosing the President, the votes shall be taken by states, the representation from each state having one vote; a quorum for this purpose shall consist of a member or members from two-thirds of the states, and a majority of all the states shall be necessary to a choice. And if the House of Representatives shall not choose a President whenever the right of choice shall devolve upon them, before the fourth day of March next following, then the Vice-President shall act as President, as in the case of the death or other constitutional disability of the President. —The person having the greatest number of votes as Vice-President, shall be the Vice-President, if such number be a majority of the whole number of Electors appointed, and if no person have a majority, then from the two highest numbers on the list, the Senate shall choose the Vice-President; a quorum for the purpose shall consist of two-thirds of the whole number of Senators, and a majority of the whole number shall be necessary to a choice. But no person constitutionally ineligible to the office President shall be eligible to that of Vice-President of the United States.

*AMENDMENT XIII*

*Section 1.* Neither slavery nor involuntary servitude, except as a punishment for crime whereof the party shall have been duly convicted, shall exist within the United States, or any place subject to their jurisdiction.

*Section 2.* Congress shall have power to enforce this article by appropriate legislation.

*AMENDMENT XIV*

*Section 1.* All persons born or naturalized in the United States, and subject to the jurisdiction thereof, are citizens of the United States and of the State wherein they reside. No State shall make or enforce any law which shall abridge the privileges or immunities of citizens of the United States; nor shall any State deprive any person of life, liberty, or property, without due process of law; nor deny to any person within its jurisdiction equal protection of the laws.

*Section 2.* Representatives shall be apportioned among the several States according to their respective numbers, counting the whole number of persons in each State, excluding Indians not taxed. But when the right to vote at any election for the choice of electors for President and Vice-President of the United States, Representatives in Congress, the Executive and Judicial officers of a State, or the members of the Legislature thereof, is denied to any of the male inhabitants of such State, being twenty-one years of age, and citizens of the United States, or in any way abridged, except for participation in rebellion, or other crime, the basis of representation therein shall be reduced in the proportion which the number of such male citizens shall bear to the whole number of male citizens twenty-one years of age in such State.

*Section 3.* No person shall be a Senator or Representative in Congress, or elector of President and Vice-President, or hold any office, civil or military, under the United States, or under any State, who, having previously taken an oath, as a member of Congress, or as an officer of the United States, or as a member of any State legislature, or as an executive or judicial officer of any State, to support the Constitution of the United States, shall have engaged in insurrection or rebellion against the same, or given aid or comfort to the enemies thereof. But Congress may be a vote of two-thirds of each House, remove such disability.

*Section 4.* The validity of the public debt of the United States, authorized by law, including debts incurred for payment of pensions and bounties for services in suppressing insurrection or rebellion, shall not be questioned. But neither the United States nor any other State shall assume or pay any debt or obligation incurred in aid of insurrection or rebellion against the United States, or any claim for the loss or emancipation of any slave; but all such debts, obligations and claims shall be held illegal and void.

*Section 5.* The Congress shall have power to enforce, by appropriate legislation, the provisions of this article.

### AMENDMENT XV

*Section 1.* The right of citizens of the United States to vote shall not be denied or abridged by the United States or by any State on account of race, color, or previous condition of servitude.

*Section 2.* The Congress shall have power to enforce this article by appropriate legislation.

### AMENDMENT XVI

The Congress shall have power to lay and collect taxes on incomes, from whatever source derived, without apportionment among the several States, and without regard to any census or enumeration.

### AMENDMENT XVII

The Senate of the United States shall be composed of two Senators from each State, elected by the people thereof, for six years; and each Senator shall have one vote. The electors in each State shall have the qualifications requisite for electors of the most numerous branch of the State legislatures.

When vacancies happen in the representation of any State in the Senate, the executive authority of such State shall issue writs of election to fill such vacancies; Provided, That the legislature of any State may empower the executive thereof to make temporary appointments until the people fill the vacancies by election as the legislature may direct.

This amendment shall not be so construed as to affect the election or term of any Senator chosen before it becomes valid as part of the Constitution.

### AMENDMENT XVIII

*Section 1.* After one year from the ratification of this article the manufacture, sale, or transportation of intoxicating liquors within, the importation thereof into, or the exportation thereof from the United States and all territory subject to the jurisdiction thereof for beverage purposes is hereby prohibited.

*Section 2.* The Congress and the several States shall have concurrent power to enforce this article by appropriate legislation.

*Section 3.* This article shall be inoperative unless it shall have been ratified as an amendment to the Constitution by the legislatures of the several States as provided in the Constitution, within seven years from the date of the submission hereof to the States by the Congress.

## AMENDMENT XIX

The right of citizens of the United States to vote shall not be denied or abridged by the United States or by any State on account of sex.

Congress shall have power to enforce this article by appropriate legislation.

## AMENDMENT XX

*Section 1.* The terms of the President and Vice President shall end at noon on the 20th Day of January, and the terms of Senators and Representatives at noon on the 3d day of January, of the years in which such terms would have ended if this article had not been ratified; and the terms of their successors shall then begin.

*Section 2.* The Congress shall assemble at least once in every year, and such meeting shall begin at noon on the 3d day of January, unless they shall by law appoint a different day.

*Section 3.* If, at the time fixed for the beginning of the term of the President, the President elect shall have died, the Vice President elect shall become President. If a President shall not have been chosen before the time fixed for the beginning of his term, or if the President elect shall have failed to qualify, then the Vice President elect shall act as President until a President shall have qualified; and the Congress may by law provide for the case wherein neither a President elect nor a Vice President elect shall have qualified, declaring who shall then act as President, or the manner in which one who is to act shall be selected, and such person shall act accordingly until a President or Vice President shall have qualified.

*Section 4.* The Congress may by law provide for the case of the death of any of the persons from whom the House of Representatives may choose a President whenever the right of choice shall have devolved upon them, and for the case of the death of any persons from whom the Senate may choose a Vice President whenever the right of choice shall have devolved upon them.

*Section 5.* Sections 1 and 2 shall take effect on the 15th day of October following the ratification of this article.

*Section 6.* This article shall be inoperative unless it shall have been ratified as an amendment to the Constitution by the legislatures of three-fourths of the several States within seven years form the date of its submission.

## *AMENDMENT XXI*

*Section 1.* The eighteenth article of amendment to the Constitution of the United States is hereby repealed.

*Section 2.* The transportation or importation into any State, Territory, or possession of the United States for delivery or use therein of intoxicating liquors, in violation of the laws thereof, is hereby prohibited.

*Section 3.* This article shall be inoperative unless it shall have been ratified as an amendment to the Constitution by conventions in the several States, as provided in the Constitution, within seven years from the date of the submission hereof to the States by the Congress.

## *AMENDMENT XXII*

*Section 1.* No person shall be elected to the office of the President more than twice, and no person who has held the office of President, or acted as President, for more than two years of a term to which some other person was elected President shall be elected to the office of the President more than once. But this Article shall not apply to any person holding the office of President when this Article was proposed by the Congress, and shall not prevent any person who may be holding the office President, or acting as President, during the term within which this Article becomes operative from holding the office of President or acting as President during the remainder of such term.

*Section 2.* This article shall be inoperative unless it shall have been ratified as an amendment to the Constitution by the legislatures of three-fourths of the several States within seven years from the date of its submission to the States by the Congress.

## *AMENDMENT XXIII*

*Section 1.* The District constituting the seat of Government of the United States shall appoint in such manner as the Congress may direct:

A number of electors of President and Vice President equal to the whole number of Senators and Representatives in Congress to which the District would be entitled if it were a State, but in no event more than the least populous State; they shall be in addition to those appointed by the States, but they shall be considered, for the purposes of the election of President and Vice President, to be electors appointed by a State; and they shall meet in the District and perform such duties as provided by the twelfth article of amendment.

*Section 2.* The Congress shall have power to enforce this article by appropriate legislation.

*AMENDMENT XXIV*

*Section 1.* The right of citizens of the United States to vote in any primary or other election for President or Vice President, for electors for President or Vice President, or for Senator or Representative in Congress, shall not be denied or abridged by the United States or any State by reason of failure to pay any poll tax or other tax.

*Section 2.* The Congress shall have power to enforce this article by appropriate legislation.

*AMENDMENT XXV*

*Section 1.* In case of the removal of the President from office or of his death or resignation, the Vice President shall become President.

*Section 2.* Whenever there is a vacancy in the office of the Vice President, the President shall nominate a Vice President who shall take office upon confirmation by a majority vote of both Houses of Congress.

*Section 3.* Whenever the President transmits to the President pro tempore of the Senate and the Speaker of the House of Representatives his written declaration that he is unable to discharge the powers and duties of his office, and until he transmits to them a written declaration to the contrary, such powers and duties shall be discharged by the Vice President as Acting President.

*Section 4.* Whenever the Vice President and a majority of either the principal officers of the executive departments or of such other body as Congress may by law provide, transmit to the President pro tempore of the Senate and the Speaker of the House of Representatives their written declaration that the President is unable to discharge the powers and duties of his office, the Vice President shall immediately assume the powers and duties of the office as Acting President.

Thereafter, when the President transmits to the President pro tempore of the Senate and the Speaker of the House of Representatives his written declaration that no inability exists, he shall resume the powers and duties of his office unless the Vice President and a majority of either the principal officers of the executive department or of such other body as Congress may by law provide, transmit within four days to the President pro tempore of the Senate and the Speaker of the House of Representatives their written declaration that the President is unable to discharge the powers and duties of his office. Thereupon Congress shall decide the issue, assembling within forty-eight hours for that purpose if not in session. If the Congress, within twenty-one days after receipt of the latter written declaration, or, if Congress is not in session, within twenty-one days after Congress is required to assemble, determines by two-thirds vote of both Houses that the President is unable to discharge the powers and duties of his office, the Vice President shall continue to discharge the same as Acting President; otherwise, the President shall resume the powers and duties of his office.

## AMENDMENT XXVI

*Section 1.* The right of citizens of the United States, who are eighteen years of age or older, to vote shall not be denied or abridged by the United States or by any State on account of age.

*Section 2.* The Congress shall have power to enforce this article by appropriate legislation.

(The foregoing is copied from an edition of the Constitution published by the National Archives and Records Administration, Washington, D.C. 1986.)

# Index

# About the Author

Bernard H. Siegan is distinguished professor of law at the University of San Diego School of Law, and the author or editor of nine books. He teaches and specializes in constitutional law. He was a member of the National Commission on the Bicentennial of the Constitution (established by the U.S. Congress) and has served as a member of President Reagan's Commission on Housing, and as a Consultant to the U.S. Department of Justice, the Department of Housing and Urban Development, and the Federal Trade Commission.

He was director of the United States Justice Department's project on the "Bibliography of Original Meaning of the United States Constitution." He was a member of the U.S. Advisory Team on Bulgarian Growth and Transition and authored its recommendation for a proposed Bulgarian constitution. He has also provided constitutional advice to government officials or private groups in Bolivia, Brazil, Canada, Armenia, Ukraine and Czechoslovakia.

Professor Siegan's most widely cited and quoted books are "Land Use Without Zoning," "Other People's Property," "Economic Liberties and the Constitution," and "The Supreme Court's Constitution—An Inquiry Into Judicial Review and Its Impact on Society."